To C Le

_I_

Temporary Soldier and Unqualified Engineer

by

Lieut. Colonel Ernest Ian Wilson Harpur

1899-1973

Memoirs of a child from an Irish Rectory

ISBN: 9798880392186
Imprint: Independently published

CONTENTS

Preface

By Sally Harpur O'Dowd

I first came across this rough draft typed copy of this book in 1988 in Schull, West Cork. My Uncle Ernest (who was my father's oldest brother) had died in 1975 and his wife Daphne gave me the said copy of his book to look at. As I recall, I stayed up late into the night reading it.

Daphne died in 2006, and in the years beforehand, not only did she hand type out her husband's book a few times on a typewriter (from his dictation), but on my recommendation, she also subsequently wrote a personal account of her experience of being married to such an adventurer (which is contained at the end portion of this book).

What occurred next was in 2007, when I was sorting through piles of paperwork and effects at my mother's home prior to her death, I came across a blue folder with Daphne's typed manuscript of Uncle Ernest's story. I took the blue folder back to New Zealand with me where it stayed until our return to Ireland in January 2013. I then thought I would get the manuscript printed for the family, but the outcome of this was an awfully faint copy, with actual words missing off pages. However, many of the family read the story and enjoyed it.

In 2020, while walking down our street in Wexford, I met a man who was a neighbour called Paul Wright (originally from

Co. Kildare). He'd spent most his life working as a radio broadcaster for Community radio in Dublin and was also an historian. Paul knew my Kildare cousins well and we became friends from that first meeting.

In 2021 I lent him a copy of Uncle Ernest's book to read. He was very inspired by the story and said it needed a wider audience, as it was a humdinger of story, as well as an important primary source historical record. After some discussion, we agreed that I would retype the original version, which took me a few months, and Paul would help with its publication. As things turned out, during the process I found a second manuscript in darker ink hidden in the aforementioned blue folder, as well as a long handwritten personal account by Daphne which was hard to decipher at first. I incorporated all documents into this second edition.

I then met up with Paul Wright again in December 2023, and he offered to edit my typed copy. As a result, he spent over a month working on the book correcting major grammar and punctuation differences, formatting the text for publication, researching all historical and engineering details, and also corroborating strange names and events. In short, nothing was too much trouble for him.

Ernest's story is riveting and as a soldier and engineer, he showed great bravery. Always seeing the fun in things, he put this down to his Irish childhood and the shenanigans he got up to. At the end of his life, it was his wish that by telling his story some engineers might benefit from his experience and avoid the pitfalls he witnessed in his career.

I find it a real privilege to be able to get this book published posthumously on his behalf, as I believe it to be an important story of historical significance.

Sally Harpur O'Dowd (his niece)

Acknowledgements

I wish to thank the following people, without whose help this publication would never have become a reality.

* Once again, Paul Wright, editor, who has been unconditional in his support for this book, and who made sure this book saw the light of day.

* My husband Dermott, for his extraordinary patience and wisdom, who offered support at every twist and turn of this project.

* My dear cousin Merrily Harpur, who validated stories about Daphne, as she had cared for her in her final years.

* Maria Rice, administrator, who always comes to the rescue without hesitation at the end of the process.

* Miriam Walker, who helped with proofing.

Chapter 1

My Early Life and Education

I am not sure when my family first came to Ireland, but Mell House Drogheda seems to have been their first home. This place adjoins Oldbridge, County Louth, where there is an obelisk to commemorate the battle of the Boyne and the tomb of Duke Schoenberg who was killed in the battle.

John Harpur was High Sherriff of County Louth. I have the old seal and parchment dated 1743, and there are also a number of letters of the same period. John was twice married, his second wife Rebecca said to be the widow of Arnold Cosby, and they had one son Singleton, born 1747. John died in 1752. As for Singleton Harpur, he became a Chaplain in the Royal Irish Artillery. I have the deed of his appointment dated 1779. He married Sarah Farris and they had about seven children. The eldest son Thomas was a scholar at Trinity College Dublin in 1802.

Staying with my ancestral lineage, Thomas Harpur married Hannah Colville and they had about thirteen children.

He was Rector of Maryborough (modern Portlaoise town in County Laois) for 40 years and built Newpark, a handsome residence, on the edge of the town. Back then, Laois was known as Queen's County. Also, in the year 1841 the population of Ireland was over 8 million people.

John Harpur was the fourth son of Thomas, and he farmed several farms near Clonroosk, Maryborough where he lived, and spent a lot of money draining the land and planting trees. He married Elizabeth Nixon, whose family's place was two miles outside Enniskillen in County Fermanagh. They had two children, my father and my aunt Anna.

My father Thomas George Montgomery Harpur, married Kathleen Wilson and they had six children. He was the Rector of Aughmacart and later Timahoe in the Queens County. My father was appointed to the parish of Aughmacart in 1896. Aughmacart in Queens County is one of the smallest churches in the South of Ireland. The Rectory was also very small, and it had not long been built. At one time there were many Priories and Castles and Towers, but in our time, they were mostly ruins.

My mother came to this place as a bride; she was Kathleen, daughter of Robert Wilson, of Castlefin, Co Donegal. She was the only surviving child of his first marriage. Her mother Kate had died when she was a child and the Armstrong cousins mostly went to Canada. Robert Wilson was a school master earlier in his life and had preached temperance all over the country. His companion was known as 'Catch my Pal' Patterson. I can remember a little bottle with a fish preserved in alcohol with which they used to demonstrate. I think the liquid was by then water – one of the young sons and myself having missed the lesson on the dangers of drink had made the changeover. My grandfather had married a second time and there was a young family growing up.

At home at Aughmacart Rectory, my sister Violet was the first child born in 1898 to our parents George and Kathleen. Within a year I was born, with the circumstances behind my birth being, one day when my father was out in the garden sowing some seeds, a maid came running saying, *"Sir, Sir the Mistress is bad, will you go for the doctor?"* My father is said to have replied, *"Tell the mistress to wait until I have finished this bed of onions."* I was born that night on May 31st, 1899.

I do not remember the Rectory very clearly, but there was a garden and 29 acres of land, which I think my father rented to a neighbour (as he was not a farmer). What I remember best about Aughmacart was that the Boyles lived at Belmont, which was less than a mile from the Rectory. Mrs Boyle was my father's sister, and the cousins were our contemporaries. Indeed, we shared a governess with them. Later when we had to go away to school, as soon as we arrived home for the holidays we would dash over to Belmont, where there was always something going on, or so it seemed.

My first school was with my grandfather, Robert Wilson, at Kenagh, County Longford. He taught about four boys, as well as his own sons and daughters. One of these boys was a son of Colonel King-Harman whose place was not far away; this lad was very popular, and he became a hero to us all, but unfortunately, he was killed in 1916 during the Great War.

My grandfather was an expert in mathematics, and we were taught Euclid as soon as we could read or write. I think I knew all the books before I was thirteen. English and Latin were subjects that I knew very little about, however we were encouraged to read and there was a good library from the old classics to Buffalo Bill and I read everything that came my way.

When I was about fourteen, I was sent to Mountjoy school in Dublin where I was not a literary success. Although I do remember some happy times and some wonderful friends, nevertheless I hated the place and have bitter memories of being beaten; sometimes for devilment, as when I exchanged the sugar at the master's table for sodium-carbonate because they had apple pie and we had rice pudding. That beating was well worth it, but when I was beaten for not knowing the Kings of England, I thought that was very cruel.

In 1906 my father was appointed to a larger Parish with three little churches and a Rectory we all loved. The parish was Timahoe in Queen's County, and the extra churches were Timogue and Luggacurran. At Timogue the congregation was often only three; one person rang the bell, one played the harmonium and sang and the third was known to walk out if he didn't like my father's sermon, or indeed if anything occurred which might not be considered 'High Church'.

Luggacurren was also a Settlers church and I think it was Lord Lansdowne who had brought a number of settlers to the place and the little church was very poor. Timahoe is about ten miles from Maryborough (modern Portlaoise town) where my great grandfather, Thomas Harpur, had been the Rector for forty years. My father George was born there and was interested in all country things and rode a horse well. I can remember sitting in front of him on a horse when there was a sudden thunderstorm. I was very frightened, as was the horse, but he managed us both well and we got home safely to Timahoe.

Timahoe Rectory, Queen's County (Co. Laois), where I was born and grew up

My ambition then was to shoot well and to get a right and a left at snipe as I had seen him do. Thankfully, many years later I could do this.

Timahoe is famous for its round tower which is near the church, and it has a very beautiful doorway ten feet up from the ground dating back to the 12th century.

I was about nine when my grandmother came to live with us, and she was very nice to us and gave me little presents. One of these was a little gold and enamel box to keep stamps in. Later when I got to go to school in Kenagh, there was a lovely lady in a cake shop who used to make special cream pastries for me. I loved her and gave her my little gold box, but my mother was not very pleased.

Granny Nixon as we called her would tell us how long ago, she could fish from the windows of her home. We had a painting of the place which is described in the old handbook as 'Nixon Hall', the seat of Alexander Nixon about two miles outside Enniskillen. In the picture there is a lake and people fishing from a boat. I often wondered how they fished from the windows, but there may have been a stream.

I still have a small round table that she gave to me – it is quite old and has a turned edge. As a matter of fact, I carved my initials on it with a penknife at the time, and my mother was not pleased about that either.

I also recall how in my youth my father bought me a football from Dublin and as he gave it to me, he said, *"All I ask is that you don't get it stuck in the chimney"*. To this I said back, *"May I kick it today?"* It was a Sunday and usually we had to be quiet, but this was a beautiful ball and I could not wait. So, going out to the front of the house I gave it a hell of a kick and would you believe it, it went down one of the chimneys and I did not know what to do. It was cold weather, and we had several fires lighting. They all smoked, there was smoke in the dining room and smoke everywhere, but I had not told anyone what had happened to the ball.

Next morning, I got out on the roof early and dropped down two boots. Nothing happened so I called my sister Edie, *"Edie, you must help me, come on."* Edie bought up one of those weights made of cast iron, which I think weighed anywhere between 14 and 28 pounds. We dropped it down the chimney with a terrifying roar and it came out in my mother's bedroom after the boots and the football. I think she was rather surprised, to say the least. I never remember her getting cross with us.

As a young lad I kept ferrets and did a lot of rabbit shooting. I had a friend called Mickie who would help me dig out the ferrets if they decided to stay down, and sometimes we could smoke them out (as Mickie knew all the tricks). Anyway, on one occasion one of my father's Parishioners died and the usual gravedigger was ill, so my father said to me, *"Do you think you could get Mickie to dig that grave?"* I said, *"Of course I can Father,"* and ran off to find Mickie. This was Saturday and the funeral was on the Sunday. I found Mickie and told him about this. My father had given me five shillings, which was a lot of money in those days, so Mickie got on with the job and it was finished on the Saturday.

On the Sunday morning, I went along about two hours before the funeral was due to arrive. I was not an engineer in those days, and so I didn't realise that this grave was too close to the little river which ran beside the church. By now the grave was full of water and I could see my poor father having to do a sea burial instead of an ordinary one! I immediately went off to find Mickie, since I knew exactly where he would be – in Bradleys pub – and by the time I had found him, he had swallowed a few pints, and he consequently walked like it.

I urgently said to him, *"Mickie you must come and help me."* So, we got some buckets and with Mickie walking like a snipe, between the two of us we managed to get all the water out of the grave, but all around looked like a swamp. When the funeral eventually came along, I held on to Mickie in case he nipped back to Bradleys; after all I had paid him money in advance for more of the demon drink!

As they lowered the coffin, I held onto Mickie with all the youthful strength I could muster, and kept saying, *"Hold on now, Mickie,"* as my father was simultaneously saying, *"dust to dust, ashes to ashes"*; even though there wasn't a bit of dust within a hundred yards of him, since it was all swamp. By now I was beginning to laugh a little bit watching my father, who could not shake the mud off his fingers. In the meantime, Mickie started to give a heave, and so I said to him, *"No, Mickie, you must wait."* I held on to his old coat tails and then when I thought it was safe, I said, *"All right now, Mickie"*, and he gave a hell of a heave with the shovel. But believe it or not, the shovel stuck and Mickie went in on top of the coffin. Being a devout Irish Catholic, Mickie naturally thought he was going to be buried by the cruel Irish Protestants and he did a sort of war dance, and in the meantime, I was laughing so much with my legs over the side that I couldn't help him out. The tears of laughter were streaming out of my eyes, while everyone else was actually crying. As you might have guessed, this was the last time my father ever asked Mickie or I to help him out in the graveyard.

There was one thing in my favour at school, I was able to play Rugby. I soon got a place on the team for the junior cup, and later I played for the Senior cup occasionally. Had it not been for the war I might have gone far in that field, but due to Kaiser Wilhelm invading neutral Belgium, this was not to be.

When war broke out in August 1914, many of us thought we should join the army. I was still only 15, so I had to wait. One day I was in Woolworths in Dublin and as it was out of bounds for us, I had put my school cap in my pocket. A rather nice-looking woman came up and offered me a white feather. I thanked her, not having the faintest idea of its significance. Maybe I looked more than 15 but I doubt it. By the way, the white feather denoted someone who was too 'chicken' or scared to fight in the war.

In those days they were singing, *"We don't want to miss you, but we think you ought to go,"* and there were recruiting concerts in the big houses and my cousin Sylvia would be asked to sing as she had a lovely soft alto voice. The Cosbys were still at Stradbally Hall and they would sometimes entertain officers from the Curragh camp. As well as the concerts, there was tennis in the summer. When I was home, I was allowed to shoot there. In fact, I remember being taken into the Gun room and being allowed to choose a gun and thought this a great honour. I have no idea whether the gamekeeper kept an eye on me. Anyway, two years quickly passed and in 1916 I eventually joined up.

Family photo taken in Timahoe circa 1920, depicting
(L to R): myself, my younger sister Grace, my mother
Kathleen, and my younger brothers Brian and Douglas

Chapter 2

Army life, Bere Island and 3rd Battle of Passchendaele

So, I was now in the army and believe it or not, subsequently spent in total seven years with the Colours and five with the Reserve. I was posted to the Royal Artillery at Port Elizabeth in County Cork. What actually happened was that as I was walking along on some street in Cork when a Major spotted me and was not impressed with my appearance. He said, *"What is your name, Gunner?"* I replied, *"Harpur, Sir,"* whereupon he looked at my putties which were in an awful mess, wound around my spindle shanks and making rain gutters.

"Are you the son of George Harpur," he asked incredulously.

"Yes, Sir."

"What have you enlisted for?" Indeed, I had begun to wonder!

I replied, *"Seven years with the colours and five with the Reserve."* He interrupted, *"Come with me, Gunner,"* and I followed him to the barracks where he tore up my papers and made me sign up for the duration of the War. I got the impression that my

11

appearance was no help in recruiting for the Royal Artillery. This man must have been a friend of my father or knew who he was.

I next went to Bere Island (the place that I remember all my life as a bad dream). There I met some of the toughest men that I have ever met. Everything I had was stolen. I think we slept on our boots to be sure of having them in the morning, as I had already lost one pair at Fort Elizabeth. A Sergeant said something insulting about my mother and I stepped out to hit him. *"Ah ha,"* he said, *"you are the sort of Gunner we want."* I was puzzled, but he put me on fatigue work rolling up barrels of beer to the Sergeants' mess. This became my main occupation, so it was with some surprise when I was posted to an Officer's course of instruction.

One or two of us felt very strongly that we must see active service before trying for a commission, so I managed to find a Captain Forsyth who agreed with me. We were able to persuade our very fine C.O. Colonel Kirkwood, and I was duly posted to the South of England for some more training. I had not been to England before, and I remember that our worst fear was that the war would be over before we got to France. I did get to France in May 1917 and my eighteenth birthday was May 31st. As it turned out, my grandfather's maths teaching was to stand me in good stead, and I was able to work out the calibration of the guns at a good speed. The third battle of Passchendaele was my awakening to the realities of war.

When I first got to France, I was still a 'sanitary orderly'. I soon rebelled against this and was posted to work out targets, which meant receiving messages about wind direction, strength and temperature. From this one should be able to work out a target in two minutes and put the guns on target in three minutes. After about one month I could do this and was posted to an Observation Post (O.P.).

Our Battery command post was in a place called Hannebek Valley. It was an old German 'pill box' and was made of solid concrete. Although the roof was originally of iron and timber, it was eventually broken up by 8-inch Howitzer shells. Most of my time was spent on Observation Post work. We had two O.P.s: one was opposite Polderhook Chateau and the other towards Passchendaele. The chateau was very tricky as it was a nest of machine guns. When observing one looked through a narrow slit and tried not to blink, because the little puffs of smoke from the guns were so quickly dispersed that it was easy to miss, and their position was vital to the battery. Sometimes a bullet would hit the steel near the slit, and this was frightening, and it was hard not to blink.

Also, we were very lucky in our battery commander 'Major Kenneth Bell'. He taught me all he knew about the calibration of guns, as well as the muzzle velocity when a shell is fired. Each gun had a different velocity and range, and Major Bell was very particular about calibration and insisted that we practice firing every gun at something that did not matter, to ascertain the correct elevation when there would be something to shoot at.

I made a great mistake one day and was told never to do it again. What happened was I got a call through from one of our aircraft and it was called an N.F, which meant terribly urgent. So, I worked out the target very quickly and got the guns on to it before any officer arrived. This was very serious and when Captain Saunders arrived, he gave me a stern reprimand and warning. Thankfully, no lives were lost, and it was a valuable lesson I learnt that day.

One part of our 'pill box' had already opened up and there was a large split in it. Some of the Anzacs had been sent to help, and when about eight of these fellows were repairing the opening of an 8-inch shell they got an almost direct hit. Captain Saunders and I rushed in to try and save these poor fellows, and though we could see no sign of wounds, they were all dying and we could do nothing to save them; so they died where they were. This was the effect of the blast.

While we attempted this rescue, Saunders got his leg splintered by a shell and he was rushed off to a dressing station, where he died within a couple of days. He was recommended for a Military Medal or D.S.O and I was recommended for a Military Medal, but nothing came of it, and Saunders died.

I remember once when I was observing in the snow, I saw a hedge and as I watched I noticed that the hedge was moving across the field towards another hedge. It was broad daylight and I suddenly realised that this was enemy Infantry moving up under camouflage, and it was only because the two hedges were getting nearer to each other that I understood what was happening. I had to signal the battery and stop that. It had been a very brave effort on the enemy's part.

Our work was mostly counter battery, which means we

were up close to the field guns. To try to break up enemy heavy artillery, sometimes we did what we called 'bombardment' to break up the barbed wire, by a creeping barrage from the far side of the wire, getting gradually closer. This was different from ordinary 'ranging', which we would use to 'shoot up' battery.

On the Ypres Salient we had a double line of triangular observation. In this way we could watch flashes and report to the battery at night and as the other O.P. would report as well, and it made for complete accuracy. Our signals came mostly in Morse and also by telephone, and when there was an N.F. sign it meant an extremely urgent target, forty rounds each gun immediately. We had six guns and each shell weighed 100lbs, which was quite something even in those days.

When I first went out, we were at Arras, and there we were only allowed to fire about ten rounds of each gun because of the shortage of ammunition. But later on in the war we had masses of ammunition. We generally used a 106 fuse, which was very fine and would burst at the slightest impact. Now I remember we had one particular fellow in the battery who thought he would get better results if he did a little adjustment. This fuse was designed so that when it spun in the air a small collar would unwrap itself. This fellow, with the best of intentions, removed the collar and in this way caused several bad pre-matures. Tragically, some people were killed before we realised what was happening. The fuse is very important, and a delayed action fuse is usually used to break up concrete.

Photo of me (front right) alongside some of my Royal Artillery comrades

At the start of the third battle of Passchendaele, we were stationed at the lip of Zillabeck lake, just outside Ypres. One day we were shelled very heavily by 8-inch Howitzers, but we did not suffer one casualty as these shells did not explode until they were well into the ground. I saw one land just beneath an officer's foot and the poor chap got such a shock that I don't think he recovered for a long time.

More of my army comrades

On Christmas day 1917 as I was coming back to the camp walking along the old plank road that ran from 'Birr' crossroads to 'Hannebek', a shell came rather too close and seemed to blow me up against an old G.S. wagon which was overturned by the side of the road. I must have been stunned as one of the ANZACS came to my help and gave me some neat rum. After I had drunk it, I could not walk so I think he must have carried me to near the camp. Anyway, I eventually arrived back at the Battery on all fours. Fair dues to my comrades, they had kept my Christmas dinner all on one plate: Christmas pudding, ham and the rest which I was able to eat through before I lay down to sleep. I must have been a horrible sight.

In France we learnt to forget some of the instructions we had learnt in England. One of these was that in action there really is no time to use the shell bearer–loader. We picked up the shell and rammed it home with the rammer and pulled the lanyard without turning round; keeping our mouths open so we did not burst our ear drums, as so many did and were deaf for years.

At one of the O.P.s I had collected a lot of hand grenades and put them in an old sandbag — they had been lying about and were very rusty. Sometime later one of our nice Lieutenants came along and gave the sack a kick and was furious when I told him what was in the sack.

By this time, we were attached to the 1st Anzacs, and I remember thinking I would get a better view if I crawled forward from where I could see Polderhook quite clearly. When I looked round, I saw an Anzac sitting nearby and I said something to him, but he did not answer. Then when I looked again to see what was wrong, I realized he was dead. 1917 was a very cold winter and this poor lad had been there for some time.

On one occasion I was sent with a fatigue party to collect vin blanc from the Estaminet, but when no one was looking, as well as the vin blanc we collected another unmarked barrel. On the way back to the dug-out we saw a sign which read: 'This way to the army church hut'. So, we collected that as well. That night a good time was had by all. Next day we were all in the most awful pain and quite paralyzed. Although we never heard what had been in that extra barrel, it was definitely potent! Needless to say, we were a very unpopular battery for several days.

We had a Sergeant Major who rather disliked the front line. He may have had a rough time before he joined us, I never knew. He and I were always at loggerheads as I had not forgiven him for making me sanitary orderly. One day when he was out of his dug-out I collected some cordite and put it in the rat holes round about. Later on, there was a frightful lot of noise, and he was very angry. He was an extraordinary fellow and sometimes after I had a long stretch at the O.P., he would call me in the night to go out to some fatigue. One night I remember in particular when I had been on the Passchendaele O.P. and was very tired. When he called me, I told him to, *"take a running jump at himself."* For this I was put on 'charge' and I had to appear before Major Bell, who said, *"Gunner Harpur 7990, you are charged with telling the Sergeant Major to take a running jump at himself."* He could hardly keep the smile off his face. Later he told me that I must never tell a 'Sergeant Major' to take a running jump at himself.

Major Bell was a wonderful C.O. and we all loved him. Shortly afterwards, I was sent home to get a commission. Major Bell had said it was my duty to the King, but I did not want to leave the battery. Like many another I had come through the Ypres Salient rather shaken. I had seen too many dead and dying men, too many rats and mud, and the horrendous devastation of France from which we thought it would never recover. I found I could not remember ordinary things or do a simple sum. I can remember hiding in a lavatory and crying my head off. I went first on leave to my family in Ireland and slept through the station where my mother was waiting to meet me. When I reached the Rectory, they wanted to burn my clothes, but it was my uniform and it had to be washed.

After some leave, I was sent back to Horsham and there I had a friend called Allen. He was boxing champion for the second army, and we had a lot of fun together. Anyway, March 17th came around and on St. Patrick's Day an Irishman is allowed to wear the shamrock. Allen and I made sure of this and found the number of the order so that when the day came, I turned up on parade with about five shillings worth of shamrock draped off the peak of my cap with its white band.

Parade was a serious business and our young lieutenant caught sight of my cap and although he could hardly see my face he said sharply, *"Take that cabbage off your hat, Harpur."* I stepped forward and said, *"Sir, according to the King's regulations numbers 1234, an Irishman is allowed to wear the shamrock on Saint Patrick's Day."* I heard a chuckle all along the line and I stepped back a proud man of eighteen years and ten months.

One time I was made a Military Policeman, which I hated, especially when I knew that Allen would have too much to drink. I saw him walking unsteadily towards the guardroom at Horsham and I said, *"Allen, Allen."* He looked around and he saw my armband with its M.P. and hit me such a clout that I did not wake up for several minutes. By then he was in the guardroom.

After some training in various places, I got my Commission. I attended lectures on gunnery and lectures on O.P. duties. I had great difficulty staying awake as I thought I knew it all. By now I was at Lydd and I remember some of us thinking we would like to go to Sierra Leone, as we had heard that we could get double pay for service there. This appealed greatly, so about six of us sent in our names to H.Q., only to be told by a staff Captain that most of the Royal Artillery had put in their names – so that was obviously off!

Chapter 3

Armistice, posted to the Indian Artillery, Iraq, leaving the army and joining the Iraq Railways

I was in London with an awfully nice fellow called Metcalf when the Armistice was signed, and in the streets we were wrapped in ribbons by some pretty girls. I was then posted to India and left in a special train for officers going east via Marseilles, and on the way, we passed some American soldiers who called out to us, *"Ah ha, ha, who won the war?"* There was no time to tell them as the train moved off.

At Bombay, Colonel Bishop was in charge at H.Q. where there were about 20 young lieutenants, but after that we were all separated out. Cliff Howes, (who I had known for a long time) was posted to Fort Agra and I was sent to the Indian Mountain Artillery at Dehra Dun. Now the Indian Mountain Artillery was something that many of us longed to get into as it was really great fun, and each Lieutenant had his own set of rules. We learned how to go into action in two minutes and the mules knew much more about this than we did. When the whistle was blown each mule would get into his position for off-loading. I thought they were really beautiful animals and I particularly remember one mule that would take the heaviest load, which was the main trunnion or cradle of the gun which weighed 450lbs, and boy, could this mule jump!

Back then I thought I must see more service as it was very important to see service. There was a rebellion going on at the Northwest frontier led by Sheik Hamid or someone, so I volunteered; but my nice Colonel Green said, *"No, Harpur, that would be quite hopeless as you have very little command of the language,"* even though I had passed my Urdu exam. I was not allowed to go.

After that I did a lot of riding in the school with a fellow called Constable. We had about 30 horses there and they had not been ridden for some time, so this was a wonderful opportunity to do something I loved – horse riding. However, this didn't last long, as I was suddenly posted to 40 Battery Indian Mountain Artillery, which was moving to Iraq with Colonel Green in charge.

During those months we did a lot of riding, as Colonel Green was mad keen to make us into 1st class horsemen and he had a riding school made out in the desert with no walls or fences. Here we would ride for hours, and after many of the usual exercises we would quit stirrups and reins. When we quit reins, that was the signal for the horses to gallop off into the desert and I would hold onto any bit of the middle of the horse to save my life. It was all rather hair-raising!

At that time, we were stationed at Daura which was a very large army camp. There was another regiment stationed about two miles away which I think were the Leinsters. On St. Patrick's Day they invited me to lunch and I took along a friend called Moss. They gave us a wonderful lunch and Moss enjoyed it even more than I thought he had, because when we galloped home to our camp, Moss forgot all about the wire fencing, but his horse remembered and stopped dead – leaving poor Moss spread-eagled across the wire.

After a few months in Iraq, we were told that all duration of war officers must return to England, so at that point my army career suddenly came to an end. I had been recommended for a permanent commission, but this had not come through, and there were some excellent fellows coming out of Woolwich who had to be considered. I was told that as I was only a 'duration of the war' officer I must be demobilised. However, I could not dream of going home without a job, as I had not had much education and work was hard to get in 1920. For this reason, I rushed around Baghdad and got the offer of three jobs – one with Public Works, another with Irrigation and yet another with the Railways. Railways offered me about 50 rupees more than the others, so I decided I wanted to become a railway man.

The army were very slow in releasing me and Railways said they could not wait forever, so I went to the army people and said, *"Look here, I will sue the war office."* In fact, I made such a nuisance of myself that they were delighted to get rid of me. Consequently, I joined the Iraq Railways, and I can remember at the time being asked by a very nice Assistant Engineer what I knew about survey work. I replied, *"Well you know, Sir, I have worked for years with a theodolite."* Indeed, I had worked with a similar thing, a No. 5 director in the Ypres Salient of all places. He was very nice about this and taking me out of the office said, *"What you really want is a job, Harpur."* I replied, *"Yes, Sir."*

"All right. I will see that you get it," he said.

I had been interviewed by Brigadier M.G. Lubbock and he passed me on to Mr. Rothers the Chief Engineer. I had left the army but most of the people in the railways had been in the army in one way or another. I was put down as an Assistant Engineer and was posted to Diwaniyah. Arriving there I was met by Lubbock, who'd been a Major and WOA M.C. and was an experienced engineer. Before the war he had worked in Canada, building bridges in the far west, and during the war he had served in France at the Dardanelles.

At this time, he was also called Assistant Engineer, and we also had a District Engineer from Canada who was a great fellow really, but with one weakness, he was rather too fond of the bottle. One day I smelt his so-called lemon squash, and it was almost all neat whiskey. Lubbock and I were worried that the sun would kill the poor fellow, so we went through his room and took away all his whiskey and spare money. At that moment he didn't care much, but after a week he came along looking miserable and said, *"My wife is terribly ill, so you will have to give me 50 rupees to send a cable."* Lubbock and I felt like criminals and naively gave him the 50 rupees.

Not surprisingly, he then shot down to the market, as he must have heard that there was a certain notorious Highland Brand whiskey on sale – which was reputedly captured from Jap stores, if I remember correctly – and was strong enough to kill a mule. After a few drinks our poor District Engineer was completely out of it, but we had learnt our lesson and thereafter kept an ever-closer watch on him. Everything went fairly well for a while, with us doing our best to keep him off the wagon; but things went south after he had to go to Baghdad to have lunch with the General, and the poor chap couldn't keep any soup on his spoon. Even though he struggled on bravely for a while after that, the general decided to give him a rest.

At that time in Diwaniyah, as well as Lubbock and myself, we had one great railwayman called Lawrence. In the neighbourhood we also had a Canadian irrigation officer whom we called 'Long cold Soda' because although he would drink our whiskey, in return he would only give us a long cold soda. This irked us, so we had to think up some way to change the situation. Anyway, the others had a brainwave and brought me into the plot, explaining what they were going to do, their basic idea being: "*When he gets out the long cold soda, you, Harpur, will pretend to be bitten by a scorpion and he will have to get the whiskey or you might die, and you must keep walking up and down.*"

We arrived at the house and were brought in and nothing much happened, so after a few minutes I said I had been bitten by an awful scorpion on my backside. I then did my best to act the part and 'Long Cold Soda' rushed off for the whiskey. As I duly walked up and down and up and down, my two co-conspirators drank the whiskey, hardly leaving me a drop.

Diwaniyah was 117 miles from Baghdad and our work was to maintain the railway line. The heat in summer would make the earth like a brick and as there was no stone ballast, in winter the earth had to be packed up and consolidated to hold the track together and in position. We also had a lot of temporary bridges over little waterways. These had to be watched, as the sand in summer would silt up, and this could cause a derailment or even a wash away.

While we were at Diwaniyah, we all practiced a lot at revolver shooting. This was primarily because we all believed (according to rumours) that a rebellion was not far away. We knew that the Arabs were well armed with guns left over by the Turks after the war. Our house was in an old Turkish fortress with enormous thick mud walls, so it was the ideal place for target practice. However, very soon there was no time for the luxury of such practice, as hostilities erupted and we fired our guns for real!

Chapter 4

Iraq Rebellion, Siege of Rumaitha, armoured trains and Fallujah

As it turned out, the anticipated Iraq rebellion began in the spring of 1920. I was at Diwaniyah with Lubbock when it broke out. At the time, even the dogs in the streets knew big trouble was brewing – with it not so much a question of if and when, but where it was going to start. As far as we were concerned it started at Rumaitha, which had a station 15 miles south of Diwaniyah, with the next station to the south a very small place called Waw.

How it began was – Lieutenant P.T. Hyatt was the Assistant Political officer and at Rumaitha one of the Sheiks had refused to pay his tax (almost 800 rupees), so he was sent by train to Baghdad; but some of his tribe shot the railway guard and the police ran away. Hyatt knew that this was the beginning and he asked for extra troops to be sent. When they arrived, they were stationed at the Serai in Rumaitha, which was a substantial two storey building with a flat roof.

At Diwaniyah we received a message that the little station at Waw was burning. Now at this stage we had not heard about the shootings at Rumaitha and would have to pass through the

Waw station to get to Rumaitha. I remember Lubbock and I left by train, and I travelled on a trolley in front of the locomotive to get a better view of the track. The only person with us on that train, besides the engine driver, was Lubbock's bearer: an Indian called Lysark, who was a fierce looking fellow who never smiled.

As we neared Waw, we could see that the track ahead was torn up so we could go no further. I decided to have my trolley lifted off the track while the train went forward, and then placed at the back so I would travel in the front on our return journey. Later, we moved slowly back towards Diwaniyah, and I had four trolley men with me. Around midnight in the clear cool air, we watched for any movement, and then suddenly out of the shadows I could see about twelve men coming in our direction. As I stopped the trolley, I noticed that the leading man in the party had raised his rifle and was pointing it straight at me. As he lifted his arm, his 'aba' opened, and I could see his white dress underneath. I fired three shots with my revolver, and he fell over.

By this time, I had had enough of the trolley, so we all got onto the train and with sporadic shooting we returned to Diwaniyah. We reached the station by daylight, and it was the hour that Lysark usually brought morning tea to Lubbock. To our astonishment he had slept soundly through the night, and arrived with a tea tray and knew nothing of what had happened in the night. We heard later that the man I had shot was a minor Sheik of the Dwalam tribe called Kesoor and he was dead.

At Diwaniyah we heard of Hyatt's situation, as Captain

Bragg with a company of Indian infantry, and myself with a railway construction company, set out with an armoured train to go to his assistance. Hyatt was a great chap and we all liked him. By this time, it was the 3rd of June 1920 and I had passed my 21st birthday on May 31st with no recollection – I felt very much older.

The expedition of the armoured train (to help relieve Hyatt at Rumaitha) was far from easy, as the track had been torn up in several places and had to be repaired before we could pass. In fact, one small bridge was badly burned and had to be made good. The station at Immam Hamza was burning, so I took a couple of my men to see if the station-master needed help. I found that he and his assistant had been murdered and mutilated. I made an attempt to catch the murderers, but the Indian Infantry did not cooperate, and I saw some men getting away. All this time our train was under fire and there were casualties in both companies.

When we reached Rumaitha we found that altogether there were about 500 men in the Serai. Besides Hyatt and his staff, we had a detachment of the 116 regiment, The Mahrattas under Captain Healy, as well as Bragg and myself with the companies we had brought with us on the train. The Serai at Rumaitha was close to the Hillah Canal and was the main building that we had to defend. There was also another place on the east side of the town which was named by the Deccan Infantry. Water was to be our first worry and later food, as the place was surrounded by hostile tribesmen and it wouldn't be easy to defend.

Hyatt heard that there were some people living about half

29

a mile to the east of town that were causing a lot of trouble and thought it might help if we could go and burn out their village. Captain Bragg was senior and therefore in command, so I spoke to him and said that I would like to go with them and take a rifle. They laughed at me, and he said, *"You are not a soldier now, Harpur."* I took my revolver and we all moved off. As we neared the village, firing became very heavy, and it appeared as if there may have been about 2000 fighting Arabs arriving on all sides. There was a system of trenches which might well have been planned by Turkish ex-officers, or it could have been that irrigation channels were being used. In any case our two platoons were overwhelmed and there were casualties. Marriot got hit in his arm, so with his rifle I took charge of the retreat.

The poor Indian soldiers were very frightened, as by now the whole place was full of Arabs and they were very close. I had to threaten to shoot at the Indian soldiers, to get them to shoot at the Arab rebels. Some of these Indian soldiers were wounded and some were dying. I knew that their rifles would be picked up and used by the rebels, so I took as many bolts as I could, making the rifles useless for the time being.

As we neared the village, the little channel we were in began to run out, but the place we were making for was still about 200 yards away. They were coming at us from all over the place, so I decided our best chance was to make a dash and we all ran as hard as we could. By now the Arabs had stopped shooting and started to rush up at us with their knives held up high. This was very frightening, and I can remember Hyatt (who was by now dead tired) saying to me, *"Shoot me, Harpur"*; as he felt sure that he was going to be captured and tortured by the men. There was a huge fellow bearing down on him, but I was able to shoot him.

Finally, we reached the place where Marriot had been with his Deccan infantry, and the place I had suggested would be easier to defend as it had an irregular outline on the roof (flat roofs and low mud walls meant there was no place to hide). When I went onto the roof, I found eight dead who had all worn puggarees and were easily seen. The rebels were only fifteen feet away by now. Then suddenly out of the blue Bragg was hit by a splinter of brick on both sides of his temple, and feeling the blood he said, *"That bullet has gone through my head."* We both managed to laugh.

The building we were now stuck at was connected to the main Serai by a narrow lane, and we knew we had to get to the Serai somehow, if we were to survive. In the meantime, Bragg had asked me to remain in charge, so I managed to cut a narrow slit in a mud wall on the roof, so we might see who was firing at us. Bragg had also agreed to leave eight men to help me, so I fired furiously from the roof to keep them guessing while the others got away.

When I thought we had a chance, I crept down to find to my horror that there was no-one there. I could hardly believe it. Then I noticed 6 bottles of beer (Bulldog brand) and I thought to myself they won't get this and loaded it into my sandbag. Then I noticed 1000 rounds of ammunition had also been left behind, so I had to decide between the two, and with great restraint I left the beer and took the ammunition!

At that juncture I crept out into the lane as noiselessly as possible and there was not a soul in sight, since no one had waited or indeed come to find me or any of our military personnel. Then I looked and saw one man coming towards me and recognized him as Mr. Mann (our Railway Supervisor) and he was carrying a Mauser revolver. I will never forget this splendid fellow. Bragg was very upset that his soldiers were too frightened to wait for me and there was no time to persuade them.

When we were all back in the Serai, we made a determined effort to see how we could best defend the place. I asked the railway masons to cut loopholes in the wall, splayed out at the back with a slit 9 inches long and 3 inches wide. I noticed one of the Sepoys making his bigger, so I crept up to warn him quietly, putting my hand on his arm saying, *"Why are you doing this?"* But at that moment he was hit by a Martini bullet and blown away from my hand – dead as a doornail!

Through another loophole I could see the palm tree where the sniper must have been, but I could not see him. In spite of the large number of rebels outside the Serai they did not attack. All the time we expected them to come in with smoke or scaling ladders, and we never knew why they didn't even try. We had 43 missing in the village, as well as 14 wounded and 2 or 3 dead. General Haldane says in his book *The Insurrection in Mesopatamia* that the Rebellion started at Rumaitha, giving the numbers in the Serai as: 4 British officers with 308 Indian soldiers; and 2 British officers with 153 Indian Railway personnel; altogether about 527 men. I did not think there were so many, but it is hard to remember.

By now food was our chief worry, as we only had rations

for a few days. Water was fetched from the river, which was dangerous as the water carriers were easy targets. I went with them on several occasions, keeping them covered while they filled up the water cans. This was not easy, and we had several casualties, as with each expedition there seemed to be more snipers shooting at us. One bullet hit the gravel near my face, and I thought I was finished. After a few more trips we decided to dig wells inside the building and surprisingly we got water at 10 feet.

From my point on the roof, I noticed a calf, and knowing we had no fresh meat I shot it. I then went down and crawled through a small hole in the wall, believing that some of the soldiers would help me to get it in. However, I had forgotten that they were Hindus and would not have anything to do with a calf. Consequently, I struggled for what seemed a terribly long time pushing the dead calf and myself through the hole in this thick wall, with my behind all the time feeling very exposed and vulnerable. Once in, there was no difficulty, though. I don't suppose the Hindus ate any of it.

There were many Arabs who were not rebellious all over the country, and there must have been thousands who only wanted to have peace restored. Among those we had Sayed Mohammed, who lived in Rumaitha not far from the Serai, who was a friend of Hyatt's and was greatly respected. We began to hope that the siege would be lifted by July 23rd. I think what alarmed us most was the thought of being captured and tortured, and we knew that many people had died in this way.

The noise of stamping round and round the fort was very weird – it was called 'housing' and it went on most of the night

– and the whole place vibrated with it. We had also heard that Colonel McVean was on his way with a column bringing food and much needed ammunition. As they approached, they were combating gunfire from anywhere between 3000 to 5000 rebels holed up in an old canal, which we could observe from our position on the Serai. Then we realised they could go no further and would have to retreat, and as we watched we could see that a sandstorm had hidden them from us, but luckily when it dispersed, they had come back. We heard afterwards that Colonel McVean had caused the sandstorm by trailing brushwood as a camouflage, which was a clever idea and it worked splendidly.

Hyatt then got word that the Sheiks would meet us to talk terms and that Sayed Mohammed would make a plan which was that Ryatt, Bragg and myself, would go out and meet Sheik Abdul Abbas, who was head of the Benne Berrais tribe. At this meeting there would be Sheik Kethithe, who was the head of the rebel tribes called the 'Walams' and the 'Dwalams'. It was agreed that at the first sign of treachery, I would shoot Kethithe (as if anyone had to be killed it must be this man). I said to Hyatt, *"This seems to me to be a tricky sort of meeting and I would like to take a rifle."* But Ryatt thought it would be better to take my revolver. Without them knowing, I put two hand grenades in each pocket (both finely adjusted to go off at a touch). I was feeling quite clever until I was confronted with a rather lively horse which was to take me to this meeting, and as the old hand grenades rattled together in my pocket, I felt sick with fright.

When we arrived at the 'mudiff' and sat down with the sheiks, Hyatt said quietly to me, *"Before you kill anyone look behind you."* I looked behind and there were three or four rifles pointed at my back. It was agreed at this meeting that Hyatt and I would go out to meet General Cunningham's Column and take these 'terms from the Sheiks'. We thought this would give us a chance, and we duly went back quietly to the Serai without any shooting.

About two days later, Hyatt and I set out for Sheik Abdul Abbus. To do so we were given two horses with very rough Arab saddles. Before long, my stirrup broke while the horse was jumping about the place, and I fell heavily and thought I'd broken my arm. I had some difficulty in mounting again with one arm and one stirrup, and then we had twenty miles to ride, as well I can remember. Sayed Mohamed had come with us, and when we went through a small place which had seemed deserted, suddenly we were surrounded by angry people. There was one man, the son of Sheik Abdul Abuss, who was very angry, since his village had been bombed.

We were pulled off our horses, and to be honest, I don't think it was very difficult to get me off. But at the time we were very alarmed, thinking we would be taken and tortured. I remember one woman tried to pull me towards her tent, but I was able to push her off with my one good arm. All this time Sayed Mohammed reasoned with the people and said prayers for our safety, over and over again. After about half an hour (which felt like a lifetime), we were released and allowed to get back on the horses. In the evening we eventually reached General Cunningham's Column.

This column had been operating in the desert for several months and had built numerous blockhouses at strategic points, leaving small fortresses manned so they could not be cut off. It consisted of about five regiments, and it was accompanied by an armoured train with my old friend Crawford Clarke in charge of the train. He was now with Railways, but previously had been a Major with an M.C. and bar. He was a great fellow.

I then went to Diwaniyah where I met a very angry General who seemed to think we had all made too much fuss at Rumaitha, and could not understand why we were so worried. I think I was able to tell him. At Diwaniyah I was able to catch up with news of the rebellion in other parts of Iraq, as Lubbock was in charge of the railway line where these armoured trains were passing. The line was torn up as quickly as it was repaired, and altogether he was having a busy time. I think he was happy to be on a horse and doing something really worthwhile. He had a good horse of his own and also a beautiful pure-bred Arab called 'Kylawn'; and with these two mounts he was able to see if the line was safe for a train to pass.

He often had to have the rails taken from behind the train to repair the track in front and let the train pass in this make-shift way. I heard that he showed great courage and could be seen galloping often under force, as there were rebels hidden in the 'nullahs' shooting at the trains. The work was very hard, and the heat was intense. I was also very concerned for my own horse.

I did not remain at Diwaniyah, and after a few baths and some food I was told to go to Baghdad *for a rest.'* This was pure fantasy, as barely had I arrived in Baghdad than I was asked to go and pull up the line to the old Doura camp, which was not far from Baghdad, as this old bridge of boats was frequently swept away. I would laugh about this with my two friends Cook and Mc Nabb, as they never knew where they would find their bridge.

Fallujah was my next assignment. It was still cut off, and not until Sept 24th did they manage to get through. I was in charge of an armoured train, and such trains had three engines with Indian drivers. These engines were small and would only pull about two trucks, but as we had about ten trucks, we hitched the three engines together to pull these heavy loads of rails and sleepers to relay the track. As well as several gangs of men who knew about track laying, we also had the Carnatic Infantry to guard us. However, I was not too pleased at the way they did it. When the train stopped at the place where track laying would begin, these soldiers would disembark and there they remained while my poor fellows went ahead laying the track. We laid as much as a mile a day and my main concern was to protect them, as the faster we went, the further we got from the Carnatics who were supposedly sent to guard us. I had a rifle with a telescopic sight, and this was put to good service.

Colonel Leachman was treacherously murdered at Khan Nucta on August 12th, 1920. This place was very remote and lay about halfway between Baghdad and Fallujah. He had been a very fine political officer who had, perhaps more than anyone, worked to keep the tribes at peace, and his murder made us feel very angry.

When the line was through to Fallujah, I was sent with

my train to repair the track between Baghdad and Mahmudiyah. There had been quite heavy fighting and the trains from the south were still not able to get through. My clearest memory of that place was finding the sleepers had been removed, and the earth put back and patted into shape so that a train driver would not notice, and his train would turn over on the embankment.

During the whole rebellion the casualties given by General Haldane are as follows:
Total for British, Indian and Allied – 2,269
Railway personnel – 23 dead and 50 wounded.
Arab casualties – 8,456
British and Indian include about 400 who were taken prisoner and tortured – most of whom died from said torture.

Chapter 5

Line to Kerbala – location and construction

After the rebellion I was back at Diwaniyah working for the railways as an Assistant Engineer. One day some friends came in and said, *"Harpur, your hair wants cutting,"* and one chap offered to cut it for me. I said rashly, *"I don't mind how short you cut it, in fact the shorter the better,"* as it was very hot weather, and I thought it might be cooler. So, one chap said, *"I will bet you 10 rupees that you will not let us shave it off completely."*

I said back, *"Of course you can and give me the 10 rupees."*

There I was as bald as a coot, and I thought it was a great joke. However, soon afterwards I got a telegram from the Chief Engineer saying he would like to see me in Baghdad. I thought to myself, *"How the hell can I explain this, they will think I have had a touch of the sun or something",* as actually all I had on my head was one small wisp of hair more or less standing up. When I got to the office feeling an awful fool, I went in to see the Chief Engineer who just looked me up and down and said, *"I think the Director had better see you."*

This was one of my first meetings with Colonel Tainah, who was most awfully nice, and they both roared with laughter at the look of me. Then they told me why they had sent for me: they wanted me to locate the line to Kerbala. Now Kerbala is one of the holy cities and every year thousands of Mohammedan pilgrims come there from all over the world. They come on camels, horses, by foot and by train.

I went to see what the country was like, as this line was to start 20 miles south of Baghdad, not far from Mahmudiya. There was a certain time when the next pilgrimage would begin, and they wanted the line ready in time. So, I went off with one or two very good Indian supervisors and a good horse. One of the Indians was Senab Gul, and to my great surprise and pleasure I met him again in Assam in 1944. By then he was a Major in Charge of a bridging company, and we went off and had a chat about the good old days.

But at that time in the early 1920's we located a good track to Kerbala, and finding out which way the sand was moving we were able to avoid the sand hills and dodge a swamp. This job was open to contractors, but their prices were so high that it was decided we should do it with direct labour. As a result, we took on about 2000 Arabs, who would make the embankment and cut through the sand hills, and all went well for a time.

Then one evening I noticed a man getting off a train near where we had our camp. I felt there was something odd about him, but could not decide what it was. In the morning there was absolute silence, the 2000 men had gone, and their tents were empty – the only people remaining being the engine driver, the supervisors and myself. I can still remember the feeling of horror that engulfed me, here I was in my very first job for the railways, and already I'd lost my work crew.

Anyway, I sent off a message to my friend Sheik Fahad of the Alziat tribe, and within a week we had enough labour to carry on. As it turned out, after about a month the men who had left with this bogus contractor began to come back. They had been badly let down and were very glad to be taken on again. I'm happy to say that we got the line through in time for the pilgrimage.

'Yours truly' with several Iraqis inspecting a railway line

While this work was going on I used to visit several Canadian engineers at the Hindiya Barracks, who were there to strengthen the old structure built by the Turks. We had met before, when I was in the Indian Mountain Artillery coming up from Basra in a paddle-steamer, and had become friends. We played poker and I lost and lost, until my luck turned, and I miraculously won back as much as I had lost. Then they said to me, *"Harpur, never play poker, you have the wrong kind of face!"* And, I have never played seriously since.

These Canadian Engineers were a very distinguished lot of officers, with many decorations including a V.C. In their mess there was an old gramophone with a horn, and Macfarlane was the owner. After a few drinks, one drink always went down the horn to make the gramophone play better. Later on, Macfarlane married, and the old horn was painted up and given a place of honour; but none of us could go in and see this without laughing. We often wondered if Mrs. Macfarlane knew what we were laughing about.

Later on, when only the Macfarlanes were there, I dropped in one day and Mac said to me, *"Harpur, you must learn to play golf."* So, he gave me some balls to practice with. Believe it or not, in my first lesson I drove all the balls into the river and poor Mac thought this was going to be rather expensive, so he gave me one of those gadgets with an 'elastic come back on the ball'. I had a few bangs with this and then giving it one hell of a crack, I hit the ground and broke the golf stick, thinking what a weak looking thing it was. In fact, it was Mrs Macfarlane's best driver! As soon as possible I rushed up to Baghdad and bought her the strongest looking driver I could find at the Hassos shop. When I produced it in triumph she said to me, *"Do you want me to play hockey?"*

As well as the Macfarlanes there was a fellow called Clinger and another called Fitzgerald, and the V.C. was Hank Smith. They were all good friends and I think all of them (except Macfarlane) were later drowned in a tragic accident. Hank was not very tall, but he was wide and strong. Later on, I heard that he'd had a bit of an argument in the Officer's club in Baghdad; at another table there was a Staff Captain who thought Hank was making too much noise, the room was on the first floor over New Street. The Staff Captain told Hank to 'Shut up'. Very quietly Hank picked the Staff Captain up by the back of his pants and his collar and walked across the floor to the open window, where he dropped him into the street below. Unfortunately, he'd forgotten that he was on the first floor, so the Staff Captain had to spend some time in hospital.

Abdulla Beg al Sana, who was the Mutasarrif at Diwaniyah, was a friend of mine and we often met. He had told me that he was in love with his first cousin who was of the Saadune family, but her family would not agree with the marriage because his grandmother had dark blood. Abdulla Beg was a splendid looking fellow. Maybe his hair was a little black, but everyone liked him. A year or so later he was promoted and was made a minister in the 'Sayed Nursi' Cabinet'. When I congratulated him he said to me, *"Do you think I could marry that cousin of mine now?"*

I said, *"I don't see why not, if you are both in love with each other."*

When he got to Baghdad and took up the new appointment, he married the girl. But his happiness did not last, as the next day her brothers came in and murdered him. He was a great loss to Iraq.

During the winter there were a lot of geese in the marshes and once when I was going by car from Diwaniyah towards Hillah, in some flooded country I could see about 50 geese on the edge of the water. I was wondering how I could get a shot at one, when along the track came an old man and a donkey. When I asked what he thought I should do, his reply was, *"Lend me your gun and one cartridge and I will bring you back two geese."* So, I did lend him my gun with a cartridge in each barrel. What happened was he got off his donkey and bending down behind the animal, he pushed it along in the direction of the geese until he got two of them in line and with one shot, he got them both. I had never seen anything like it in my life.

About one year after the rebellion, I was in charge of the labour on the railway line from Diwaniyah to Hilla. As there was some difficulty about a train, I decided to go by horse to see what was happening and left early in the morning. The weather was very hot and by about 11 am, I was very tired and so was my horse, since riding along the track was more difficult than I thought, and the distance was 50 miles. I was carrying about 2000 pounds in Rupees, mostly paper money, but still quite heavy. If that wasn't bad enough, I also carried a heavy revolver.

In the distance I could see the palm trees near the Hilla canal and knew I must have water. Getting off my horse and walking into a small village, an old man came out and greeted me in the usual way, *"Peace be to you"*; to which I replied, *"Peace be to you."* Then he said, *"Please excuse me, I cannot shake hands, as*

44

one of your bombs has withered my arm. My name is Sheik Abid." I said, *"Sheik Abid, I am very sorry about your arm, and I am very tired and so is my horse. Will you take care of my revolver and this money and allow me to rest here for a few hours?"* He agreed and could not have been kinder.

This poor little family took me into their mudiff, the women threw water over the reeded roof to cool it for me, the air was burning hot, and a slight sandstorm was blowing. They killed a chicken and cooked it for me while I slept, and when it was ready, they gave me a lovely meal. All the time I knew that the money would have kept him in comfort for the rest of his life, but I went safely on to Hilla (with all my valuables) after a few hours. I lived among the tribes that I had fought against, and they knew all about it, but I shall never forget their kindness.

Chapter 6

Bridge over the Euphrates at Barbuti

In 1924 M.G. Lubbock asked me to go down with him to Barbuti where we would build a bridge across the Euphrates. I was very pleased about this as Lubbock was a very experienced engineer and I knew I would learn a lot. The site for the bridge was near the main line and upstream of the old bridge, and it was to be the first permanent bridge over the Euphrates. The country all around got flooded every year, though not in the immediate vicinity of the bridge. The new bridge would consist of 5,100-foot spans, and one lifting span to allow boats to pass up the river, which would be a 40-foot Bascule.

Lubbock planned the concrete layout with much care, and it would deliver concrete at the rate of two tons each minute. His plan was to build a structure which would take three large hoppers, and at the bottom of each hopper there would be a concrete mixer. From the top of the structure a crane would lift sand, gravel and cement and would then deliver to the hoppers. These in turn would empty into the mixers, and when ready, into tip-wagons for delivery to the piers. We began work in 1925 by first building a temporary bridge of timber piles with bracings and no. 1 beams and a track for tip-wagons. This was used throughout the construction to deliver materials to the six piers. It was high enough for the small ships to pass underneath, and the spans were about 25 feet.

Lubbock was tall and thin with a cryptic sense of humour and sometimes he would be silent for hours. I was about 10 years younger than him, and I used to think he was angry about something until one day he said simply, *"I never talk unless I have something to say."* Eventually I got used to his silences and I respected his judgement enormously.

Bill (M.G.) Lubbock holding two dogs in Iraq

Barbuti was not far from where I had been during the 1920 Rebellion. The tribe nearby was the Alziat and the two Sheiks belonging to this tribe were old friends of mine. As mentioned earlier, I had often visited them when I was inspecting from Diwaniyah, and it was always a pleasure to call in on them and hear their news.

As well as M.G Lubbock and myself, there was a senior foreman Khan Singh, a Punjabi Sikh, who was a wonderful person with a very white beard and a benign countenance. These warlike people had beautiful manners and a noble bearing. Khan Singh was assisted by some Indian skilled staff, Pathaan riveters and Bombay Khallossies. The labour was made up of Arabs, Kurds and Assyrians, altogether about 80 men.

Lubbock's plan was to erect the girders on land and float them into position with pontoons, which was a comparatively new method in those days, with each girder weighing about 150 tons. To do this, we began by putting three separate railway tracks down on the site, with a truck on each track. We then placed one leg of a three-legged derrick in each truck, and we were able to use this throughout the construction for the erection of the girders. By doing this we saved having to build another temporary bridge.

These girders had a 1-inch camber, and it was a simple matter to achieve this on the ground. In this way we were able to sink the piers and erect the girders at the same time, saving months in working time. The construction of the piers was what is called 'open caisson'; by this we mean the use of grabs inside the wells, and as the earth is drawn up, the caisson sinks down. Particularly in sand where there may be pockets of soft sand, one has to be very careful not to sink too far, as well as not to sink under water level. As these caissons had to go down 30 feet below the bed of the river, and the margin of error allowed was about 5 inches, our instrument work had to be very accurate, and the levels were extremely important. As a result, there was always some anxiety as these caissons were being sunk, since the pier would be of little value if the error was excessive.

I can distinctly remember how the no. 5 pier gave us a lot of bother. When several no. 1 beams cantilevered out when loaded with kentledge weights, we had to use water jets to pull the caisson straight. Near the end of the sinking, no. 5 was most important, because if the loading exceeded the weight – in this case 4 ½ tons per square foot – by going too deep, then the whole bridge would be endangered.

In addition, when the correct depth had been reached, a very important operation was plugging the caissons. These had to be plugged with about 8 feet of concrete, and this could not be disturbed for about a week. Also, this had to be kept absolutely watertight. Now various methods of procedure have been used over the years to achieve this. In the old days the method was a diver went down, and the concrete was delivered through a pipe, but it was often found that the diver's movements could spoil the strength of the concrete. At Barbuti we used a more modern method called a 'bottom dumping box'. This is well described by Fowler in his book *Sub-Aqueous Foundation*, and also by Jacoby and Davis in his *Bridges and Foundations*, which in my humble opinion are perhaps two of the best books ever written about bridge building.

This box is designed with two stiff sides extending below the bottom. When the boxes touch the bottom of the well and the weight is taken, the other sides will open up like doors and the concrete will be deposited at the bottom of the well. The box is then removed slowly, not to cause a rush of water which might move the concrete just placed. This box must be as large as possible to allow for slipping comfortably into the well, and also placing the largest amount of concrete at each operation.

Usually, the water level outside will be the same as inside until this seal is complete, and the caisson has been pumped dry. A thorough examination is then possible in case of the slightest leakage, which would have to be sealed. When the bottom plug is absolutely correct, our practice was to fill the well with sand. I was never sure that this was sound, but it was an accepted method. I think that the correct moisture content is nearly impossible to obtain, and that this added weight was an unnecessary hazard. However, we filled with sand, and put on the top plug, incorporated with the shape of the pier to achieve the 50 degrees cutting edge up and down stream to minimize scour; with these being shaped to the top, then gradually reducing in size, where they would finally take the weight of the girder.

Placing the girders on the pontoons was tricky as the loading had to be absolutely in the centre. Each girder would take three pontoons, and to get them on to the position, we made spans with no. 1 beams bolted together. Then with timber bracing on each span, we fixed rails on which we slid the girders onto the pontoon. The whole manoeuvre was worked with cranes and winches. One major anxiety was to make sure that the pontoon would not stick in the mud. We took no risks and a survey showed that the river was 20 or 30 feet near the centre, but near the bank there was only about 6 feet of water. We also knew in flood this river could rise as much as ten feet in a few hours and there was considerable silting.

To make a drag scraper, this is made of three curved rails and a steel sheet connected by cables to a steam winch on the other side of the river; and by going backwards and forwards this lowered the bed of the river, and in this way we knew that the pontoons would stay afloat when loaded.

Believe it or not, the floods were not caused by rain, but instead by melting snow in the faraway Persian mountains, with seldom any warning. On one occasion the flood caused by such mountain snow melt rose so quickly, that we had to work extra shifts to keep the caisson walls above the rising water, and Lubbock's concrete layout proved steadfast and rock-solid.

Oddly enough frost was another hazard. I remember how one particular year we had a very severe frost, and pipes and valves were broken as if they had been hit by a hammer, and icicles hung everywhere. It was all most unusual, and again with no warning whatsoever.

Needless to say, in a hot country like Iraq heat was of course our real worry, and one thing we really had to guard against was any delay when the concrete was in the tip waggons, as it would begin to quickly set and become useless.

For this reason, the track on our temporary bridge had to be well laid and maintained.

To anchor the pontoon, we drove piles to the bottom of the river with a false pile following. These were attached to buoys by wire ropes and could withstand any flood. The pontoons were also held with cables to the buoys. At the end of the work, it was a simple matter to release the wire ropes from the piles, so as not to interfere with shipping.

Later when I went to London and called on the Crown Agents for the Colonies, I told them about the Barbuti Bridge showing them some of my photographs. They were very complimentary and also surprised that Lubbock and I, with a few Indian foremen, could build a bridge like this and finish it in two years (1925-26). The consultants were Rendel Palmer and Tritton, and they must have had complete confidence in us as we never saw them.

While this work was in progress Lubbock came in one day and with a curious expression on his face, he said, *"My wife and daughter are coming out for the winter."* I knew that Mrs. Lubbock had been spending the winters at Aix les Bains, and when I thought of the primitive conditions we lived in at Barbuti, I felt a shiver run down my spine, as I knew our spartan accommodation would require some work, to become more acceptable. I said, *"We had better get busy and build on some more rooms."* *"Yes, yes,"* said Lubbock, *"and Khan Singh will see to that."*

These mud houses were easily built, the bricks were made and left in the sun to bake, and after a week or so the building began. In this case we put glass in the windows, since up to now we only had wire netting to keep out the bats. However, as we each had our own bathroom, it meant building at least one more. Everything went smoothly with building the extra bathroom, until at the last moment it was decided to paint the bath itself. This was a slow drying paint with disastrous results. I'll diplomatically say no more!

One local Iraqi man I met in 1926

Chapter 7

Rabies, malaria, marriage, hydro-electric scheme on the Shannon, and railway bridge at Quaraghan.

We had many visitors at Barbuti. Sometimes people would come by train and sometimes they would arrive by aeroplane, landing in the desert nearby. Amongst these visitors was my cousin Dermot Boyle (from my Aughmacart, Co. Laois childhood), who was with the R.A.F stationed in Baghdad. I think he was a Flight Lieutenant at the time and later became the head of the Royal Air Force. Anyway, he came down and stayed with us for a few days. He was rather intrigued by my motorboat and having got it out of the mud where it had buried itself, he made it work better than it had ever done before.

We each had our names over our doors and Dermot thought this was rather a joke. In small letters under Mr. Harpur he wrote 'dentist'. I imagine this was the most unlikely profession he could think of for me at the time.

We were able to shoot partridge and duck, as well as snipe in and around Samawa, which was our nearest station. The market there was a wide-open place, where the camels would come and offload their merchandise, and then load up with all the necessities: sugar, tea, coffee and whatever else the market provided. This was not much, and I distinctly remember how the market's main meat stall would be black with flies; with live chickens sitting about tied up, ready to be sold and eaten in a shorter time than bears thinking about.

In addition, there would always be a chap going about with a goat skin full of 'liban', which was a sort of yoghurt which he would pour out through one of the legs into a tumbler, and then sell as a drink to a thirsty passerby. I can't remember that the tumbler was ever washed, but sometimes we would see him washing the goat skin at the bank of the river – filling it up and kneading it out again, with an expression of a surgeon sterilizing his knife.

At the time, the famous Gertrude Bell was advisor to the High Commissioner, Sir Percy Cox. She was a fluent Arabic speaker, and knew more about the tribes than anyone, since she had been travelling all over the country for years. I was sent to get her help on one occasion, when I was very worried about some rumours I had heard. The rumour was that the Dwalim tribe had sent their women away because they believed they were going to be bombed for not paying their taxes. After I told her what I knew, she asked me to go and see them at A.H.Q. I can remember the A.V.M. was on leave, but I did see his next in command. I think their maps were not very accurate, and the area marked 'desert' was in fact cultivated country, and people were living there. I said to them, *"This sort of bombing could start another Rebellion."* The operation was called off, and my friends Sheik Fayed and Braed were always thereafter grateful to me.

55

I do not remember when I first got malaria, but I think it was at about this time. In those days the treatment was massive doses of quinine, several aspirin, a stiff whiskey, and into bed with a great weight of blankets. Miritch (my Arab bearer) would see to this and leave several pairs of pajamas to change into as the fever broke, and I sweated to get rid of it. These attacks would come on with little or no warning, but were often connected in some way with an emotional upset.

Rabies was always a fear in Iraq, and we had all read P.C. Wren's book *Father Gregory*, but it is only when it happens to oneself that the full horror of it really hits home. We all kept dogs, and I had one lovely dog named Con – an Irish wolfhound – that I had taken out to Iraq. He slept in my bedroom and had his own bed, as he was nearly as big as I was. Among the other dogs was an Airedale terrier, and this dog got rabies and had to be destroyed. We then discovered that he and my wolfhound had been together all night. This was serious and we were all hoping that it would go no further. Unfortunately, when the trains stopped at Quaraghan station, passengers would get off to stretch their legs. Now as it happened, some rather particular people getting off and seeing dogs and then hearing about our anxiety, duly complained to the authorities. As a result, all the dogs in the district had to be destroyed. My dog Con and several old friends of ours were shot, and it was one of the bitterest moments for me. We heard afterwards that it had been at another station that suspect dogs were seen.

Twenty-seven people had to go to Baghdad for the treatment, and we got daily injections in our stomachs for about (I think) three weeks. We were told not to have any drinks; and this was given emphasis by vivid descriptions of rabies-infected-men barking like dogs, and growling like wolves, in their last hours. We were a very depressed lot and I do not remember much fun during this period.

At about that same time my father, who had been ill, died in Ireland and as I was almost due for leave, I went home earlier than planned. I am sure I was a bit of a wreck, as I frequently got bouts of malaria. Arriving back to my native Ireland, I wanted to see any interesting engineering that was being done at that time, so I took some time out to visit the Shannon hydro-electric dam scheme near Ardnacrusha in County Clare. This was to supply electricity to southern Ireland. A German firm had been invited to do the construction, and they had brought their families with them, as well as (from what we heard) much of their own food as well.

I was shown the plans for this hydro-electric scheme, and to my amazement there were no records of trial borings having been taken. I heard later that this cost Ireland quite a lot of money because they had run into unexpected rock formation in one of the channels (the Tidal Race).

Also, during this visit home I met the girl I was to marry. Although I'd fallen in and out of love several times before, this time it was for real. How it occurred was, my mother started telling me about a girl called Daphne McLean, who lived near my sister Violet at Stradbally in County Laois. The minute I met Daphne for the first time, I saw at once that my mother was right, she was just my type. Although Daphne's family were old friends of my family, she and I had never met. The

McCleans had come to live at Kellaville, County Laois after the war. It had been a beautiful old place, but was badly in need of a lot of things. In spite of this, it still possessed a certain charm and glory, and the family was a happy one, and particularly loved playing tennis and swimming in the lake during the summer. At that time, it was spring and point-to-point races were going on all around this hunting country, so we took picnic baskets and went to watch these races with friends and relations. It was the greatest fun and we got engaged.

I celebrated my engagement with a severe attack of malaria and had all the usual treatment from my fiancée and her family. The family were rather stunned by the whole procedure, and tales of wars and boars did nothing to reassure them. There was a lot of teasing, and someone would ask her, *"What are you going to do in the desert with sand in your tea?"*

I don't know what her answer was, but all went well, and a marriage was arranged for the last day of August 1927. As I had been abroad since I left school, I did not know much about these formal occasions. Everyone was talking about formal clothes, and I had very few such clothes to hand. Anyway, when we went to England to stay with various relations, I bought a Moss Bros suit for the wedding. I had to buy a top hat, white spats, and white kid gloves which I never wore again. The suit still hangs in my wardrobe, and I have worn it dozens of times since then.

We had a large wedding at Kellaville, and our brothers and their friends packed confetti into every possible inch of the car and our suitcases. We heard afterwards that it was 'pure luck' that someone was caught in the act of putting confetti in the petrol tank, and was removed bodily. As for the honeymoon, we toured Connemara for about 10 days and had a lovely time there.

We then sailed from Trieste for Beyrout on a ship named the 'Lloyd Triestino'. The ship called at Alexandria and from there we went down to Cairo and saw the Tutankamen treasures at the museum. They had not long been on show. At Shepheard's Hotel in Cairo, the huge slices of pink melon in rows on ice, looked a lot better than it tasted.

Despite September in Cairo being rather hot, we paid a visit to the pyramids, where the guides begged to drag us to the top, up those 3 feet blocks of stone. We walked along one side of the 12 ½ acres covered by Cheops. Now I had been to Egypt before, but it was a lot of fun showing it to my bride who had never been abroad. From Beyreut over the Lebanon to Damascus, the markets there were always interesting, with endless silks, brocades, beads and jewellery.

By this stage in our honeymooning, we had very little money left, but we were still able to buy some nice things, since in those days the 'word of an Englishman' was good for credit and it was very welcome. I distinctly remember we ate crystalized fruit in the street called 'straight'; and saw the tomb of John the Baptist in one of the Mosques, which the guide treated with great respect. He also surprised us by saying that one particular minaret would not be used again, until Jesus Christ came back to earth.

I had a rather elaborate camera – a box affair with plates

– and at every border customs, officers insisted on saying it was a typewriter, and refused to hear otherwise. Syria, Palestine and Iraq were French and British mandates at that time, so it was much easier to travel there than Egypt, with no confusion about cameras.

After a couple of days, we were sorry to leave Damascus with its camels and donkeys, dance halls, garish electric light, as well as its lovely scent of orange blossom and jasmine – with here and there a tinge of paraffin – and also a strange mixture of East and West. From there, we travelled about 600 miles to Baghdad, with the wide track (12 miles in places) running through the desert all the way; and with us motoring along in a four-car-convoy for safety, since there was always a danger of the Druses raiding.

Once the olive and orange groves were left behind, there was a line of bare hills and very soon the horizon encircled one and was featureless as far as the eye could see. Rutha was the first stop, and it was called a Rest House. There was a good meal at 9 pm, and the tables were decorated with sauce bottles of every variety known and also many we had never heard of. After a short rest we left again at midnight, since it was easier travelling in the night. Trying to keep awake or trying to go to sleep was equally impossible. We had all our baggage with us in this enormous car and we could almost stretch full length at the back. In addition, we had to be sure that the driver did not go to sleep. He was either Lebanese or Assyrian and I talked to him in Arabic.

After Rutha, our next stop was Ramadi on the Euphrates, and already the day was very hot. There was a kind of breakfast waiting with a smell of cooking, not bacon and eggs, but lamb chops (with a smell of goat) and brewing coffee!

It was late afternoon when we eventually got to Baghdad, tired and covered with desert dust, except for the eyes which had been shaded with sunglasses (with side pieces to keep out the sand, thus leaving our eyes red). We went to the Maude Hotel near the old Maude Bridge. The hotel had: baths, where the water ran into a trough before finding a drain; and mosquito nets, which made the beds look like four-posters; and the Tigris River at the edge of the terrace, with tables set for dinner, waiters in long white robes and bare feet moving about silently, as well as men cooking fish on charcoal by the water's edge.

One could also see the bridge of boats spanning the river, swaying a little in the breeze (or up and down sometimes in a curve), the passengers being men, some attired in white robes and others in brown. One also witnessed mullahs and priests representing all the eastern churches; women looking like black tents in purdah; camels and donkeys laden with melons or oranges or firewood or kerosene tins; and horses ridden by very important looking gentlemen in long robes with gold or silver embroidery.

Mingled with this cavalcade there were cars from all parts, the old T. model Ford was still to be seen, and the big desert-going American tourers, pushing along behind a camel or being nudged by a little donkey. Also to be seen were high seats near the Cafes where the men sat and talked and smoked their pipes through a bowl of water (which was called a 'hubble-bubble' and was passed along from one to another);

gramophones with horns blared out an Eastern noise; and women occasionally passing in their black robes, their faces covered, as they looked out through a panel of gauze. The children had red lines around their eyes and sometimes a bead stuck to their foreheads; and when one looked at a baby's face, the mother would wave her hand to beat away the flies, which often covered the poor little mite. This was Baghdad in 1927!

Once back in Iraq, I was posted to bridge-building duties in Quaraghan, which is a station one hundred miles north of Baghdad. The bridge being built was near the station and the engineer's bungalow was beside the river Diala. The bridge was to replace the old railway bridge, and the method being used was rather different from the procedure at the Barbuti bridge. George Gillies was the assistant and R. G. Lubbock was in charge. When I arrived the caissons were being sunk, but this time the method was pneumatic sinking, which means that the wells are kept dry under pressure; with men working down in the wells, watching the grabs. These men had to come up very slowly, the speed of their ascent depending on the depth, as they were in danger of something called 'Bends' (similar to diving).

I was in charge of riveting up the girders, and to do this I had a gang of Pathans, a tough bunch. On one occasion a red-hot rivet was dropped on my hat by someone who must have thought I was too fastidious. These girders were not floated out as at Barbuti, but were instead erected on railway bogies. This was because there was not enough depth of water except in high flood.

The country around Quaraghan was hilly, and in the

spring these hills were covered with little flowers: all the little annuals that grew at home, here they were miniatures, linaria, stock, antirrhinum, wallflowers and many others all growing in a splendid herbaceous mass. On the hills nearby there were drifts of small red tulips and bright red anemones, which (if I remember correctly) had blue centres and made a wonderful splash of colour. The flowers had a very short season between the end of winter, which was very cold up there in the hills, and the beginning of spring which would soon be very hot and dry and would burn up all the little flowers. Nearer the foothills there were acres of small blue iris, and coming on these in this colourless land was unforgettable.

From Quaraghan we could see the Persian mountains covered with snow in winter; and in between there was a wide stretch of rolling country, and here the camel-breeding nomad tribes would move about in search of pasture for their animals. Sometimes the whole tribe would have to cross the river and travel many miles for feeding.

While the bridge was being built one of these migrations took place, and as they were anxious to cross the bridge, we organized a timetable which would not interfere with the trains or the construction of the bridge. There was a few days delay, and they sat about near the bridge, where we could see them from the house. At last, the day came when they could start crossing, and they happily streamed over all day long, camels laden with belongings – women and children, hens and sheep, all up on the camel in a sort of wooden frame, swaying from back to front and from side to side. It would be hard to imagine a more uncomfortable way of travelling, but they had always done it this way, and they would keep on for mile after mile. The whole procession took two weeks to get over and we were absolutely fascinated watching it.

When the bridge was finished, I was sent to Baghdad to be a P. A. to the Chief Engineer, Mr. Heinneman, and we stayed in Baghdad for about a year. This was all very different from anything I had done up to then. Although life in Baghdad was good fun for a short time, nevertheless as soon as I saw a chance of getting back to the desert, I asked to be sent there.

The social life in Baghdad primarily entailed calling and leaving visitor cards on the people who had been there before us (who waited to be called on by us 'newcomers') – writing our names in the book at the Residency and waiting to be invited to some reception. The Alwiyah club was very popular, with tennis, a bathing pool, a ballroom and all the usual club facilities. I suppose the Air Force Ball was the big event of the year, and then there was usually a fancy dress affair, which I can remember going to as an 'arabanchi'. I wore the usual Arab costume with a forage cap on top of the chaffia (this they did to show their independence). Commodore Cosby (my old childhood friend from Stradbally Hall in County Laois) came with me, and we drove to the club. I think he sat at the back of the car dressed as some sort of brigand, and our disguise was so good that we were not allowed in! Eventually the 'arabanchi' came and claimed his horse and I removed my headgear; it had been a lot of fun.

We slept in the garden all through the hot weather, as it was very pleasant under the palm trees. Most people dined out, with tables and chairs all carried out onto the lawn, and lighting at a distance to keep off mosquitos and sand fly. However, a flit gun would be at hand, and we would squirt it under the table from time to time, since sand fly fever was very unpleasant, rather like a bad 'flu'.

During this period Public Works were also building a bridge over the Tigris at Falujah, so M.G. Lubbock and I went out to have a look at the work which was being done by an English firm of contractors, and their agent took us around. During the tour Lubbock asked if he could see the trial borings, and they showed nothing but sand. Lubbock then asked if we might see the pile driving records, as these piles were being driven for the temporary bridge. The records showed that the piles stopped suddenly, and from this it seemed to us that they were not in sand, but in sandstone; and that there were outcrops of sandstone in the vicinity. We came to the conclusion that the borings had been done incorrectly, and we thought it should have been a diamond drill bringing up a full core. Lubbock was very anxious about this, and he told the Public Works people.

This was quite a large bridge, and (in my memory) comprised seven spans (each 150 feet), and during the construction they were using the steel for the permanent bridge in the temporary work. Unfortunately, when the caissons were commenced, they soon ran into sandstone and the open caissons would not sink. Since there were no means of converting to pneumatic sinking, the work continued with grabs, but because there was not enough penetration, the floods rose and before anything could be done, the whole thing was swept away. In a nutshell, the bridge was a complete loss!

The blame lay with the wrong method used in taking these trial borings before the bridge was designed. Pile driving requires a lot of experience; and the fellows with the percussion rig should have known by the way the pile sinking stopped suddenly, that it was not sand but sandstone that they had run into, even if the trial borings had not told them so. I learned a lot from this and pile driving – and consequently trial borings have always been of paramount importance in my engineering life.

Chapter 8

Wild boar hunting in Iraq

Colonel Bromiloy came to Iraq as Cavalry advisor to the Iraq army. Since he had done a lot of boar hunting in India, he was keen to start the sport in Iraq. There were many wild boars in the marshes, and they did a lot of damage to the crops. The people were frightened of them, some children had been killed and the Arab would shoot them when they got the chance. These big boars would measure as much as 42 inches at the shoulder, and they would run like mad. It was hard to catch up with them even on a good horse. They had a clever way of jumping sideways over a ditch without taking a run at it.

The net result of all this was the Baghdad Boar Hunt was started, and Lubbock and I joined it with various other people, including officers from the Iraq army (both British and Iraqi), and some R.A.F. personnel. Among the civilians was 'Brough Sadler' who managed the Eastern Bank; he was a great friend and a good horseman. He was also 'Master of Hounds' for the Exodus Hunt which hunted around Baghdad, meeting at places like Daura Camp and Cetesephon. Jackal and foxes were the usual quarry, and it was nice open country for a good gallop. However, we thought that pig sticking was more exciting. Brough Sadler did both, when they were not arranged for the same weekend.

Lubbock and I knew this country better than most of the others, since we had ridden over large areas, looking for good shooting country with duck or partridge, and asking about pig. There was always great excitement when we told the people that we would come and kill their pigs, and actually we often hunted for days without seeing even a trace of a pig, quite apart from catching up with one.

The rules for this sport were that only boars were killed, and not more than three people would go after any one boar. I need hardly say that these rules were not always kept. Oddly enough my most distinct memory is the act of spearing the boar, with the aim being to kill him in one stroke. To do this was a matter of timing and having the horse ready to charge in as the pig charged. If one got the timing wrong, then the danger was that the horse might be gored, or indeed the rider (if the horse fell); and I myself had one or two very lucky escapes.

While thinking back in order to write this chapter, and talking about it to my wife, she suddenly said, *"I never remember you getting any pleasure out of killing the pig. How is it that you can't cut the head off a fish now?"* My reply was, *"I would not be on a horse."* However that may be, I think it had something to do with the hours and hours spent hunting, and then miles and miles of gallop after an angry boar who would have a root at anything that got in his way. Once in my old Ford car an Arab woman called out, *"Pig, pig,"* and to my astonishment the pig charged the car. I had to pull sharply away to avoid the car being gored in the mudguard.

The Boar Hunt usually started out in the early hours, when it was still dark, and rode out sleepily to some place where we heard there was a boar. On one dark morning at Belad Ruz, as I was riding out over the little bridge, my horse hesitated to scratch his chin with his back foot, and I fell off on the other side which made everyone laugh. Belad Ruz was unique in many ways, as it was a very large estate owned by some Greeks and managed by a Dutch man P.C. van Scherpenberg, whom we called 'Beg' (which was a local title of respect). Belad Ruz was in the middle of a palm and orange grove, its main house with its thick mud walls was hidden by trees, and around it's high walls sat 'Haji Lug Lugs'. These were black and white stork, which made a fearful shindy clattering their long beaks together, while they stood about guarding their nests, or just coming and going like patients at a dispensary.

There was a wide balcony on two sides of the house, where extra guests could sleep, and there was also a vast room away from the house where people camped in comfort. Upstairs there were several bedrooms which all opened on to the saloon, where a lot of fun and ragging took place after a long day. Once on St. David's Day we had Captain Bamfield, and he belonging to a Welsh Regiment was allowed to say, *"and St. David"* as often as he could fit it into the ordinary conversation. This got a bit tedious to the English, Irish and Scots, not to mention the Dutch (who understood it even less than the rest of us); so, we all sat on him, but from underneath a heap of bodies we could still hear *"and St. David."* Mrs. Lubbock thought this had really gone far enough and with a soda siphon she was able to put a nice cool end to a lot of fun.

I don't think I can improve on the description in the hog hunters Annual for 1933 when I won the Bromiloe cup: *"There were sixteen this year, and after the preliminaries, five were left in for the semi-final heats; three Iraq army officers and two Britishers. The first semi-final produced a first-class heat. They went top speed and finally Lubbock speared when all three were abreast.*

The other semi-final between Mahmoud al Rindi and a previous winner Harpur, was won with a shade of luck by Harpur who was crossed by the sow. After Mahmoud had been just on, Harpur fell in spearing, but retained his spear. The final therefore was between two members who have done more regular pig-sticking than anyone else here in the last ten years. In the run-off, Lubbock was on first but missed letting Harpur in, who speared heavily. I think Lubbock was almost as pleased as the winner".

Lubbock had already won the cup twice. Later when I was posted to Basra, I did more boar-hunting than I had done all along, simply because there were hundreds of wild pigs. I often went alone with my 'Syce' (horse), as there were not many people interested. Once or twice, I found someone who wanted to come out, but then I would have to lend him a horse. My best pony was an Arab stallion called Bonzo, who was as brave as a lion, and I am glad to say he only once got a slight scratch.

Chapter 9

Baghdad, collapse of bridge at Falluja, and being posted to Basra

We had been at Diwaniyah for four years and as my work was to maintain the track between Baghdad and Samawa, it entailed me having to spend about half my time out on inspection sleeping out in a saloon. In winter this was quite pleasant, but in summer it was extremely hot. Of course, my wife could not come in the hot weather, which meant that she was often quite alone. However, since there were two sentries, who were great fellows who walked about through the night, carrying rifles, I knew that she was quite safe.

This was alright for a time, but we often thought that there must be other places to live and work, and, of course, I always hoped for another bridge to build. When Alec Holt was made acting chief engineer, he promptly sent me down to Basra, and while this was certainly a change, it was not thought of as a favour. This was because the work was very much the same as I'd been doing before. This time I had to maintain the track from Samawa to Basra, about 180 miles up through Ur of the Chaldees. At the time Sir Leonard Wooley was at Ur.

I had always been interested in these digs, but going

around with Wooley was a totally new experience, since he had a wonderful way of seeing the history of it, and what was more, he could make me see it too: *"There was the street where Abraham must have lived, here is the house with its mud brick walls and small cooking place. Here is a collection of pots and dishes, here are the tools they used and the chimney and perhaps the residue left by Noah's flood."* It was all quite fascinating. There was nothing else of interest to be seen all the way to Basra and, believe it or not, only one tree!

The port of Basra at Margil was fairly important. Colonel Ward was Port Director, and he was knighted later on. They had a nice house on the Tigris, a lovely garden and tennis court where we used to play when invited. Also, the Royal Navy came in at regular intervals. At that time there were four sloops in the Persian Gulf, and while we were in Basra, we had a visit from the Indian Ocean Fleet which included the D. class destroyers and a light cruiser.

We had several friends among these visitors, and we looked forward enormously to their coming, since it was like a breath of fresh air. Naval officers are not renowned horsemen, but they seemed to enjoy riding out into the desert. We still had about three horses which we could lend them, and we could usually find some others from our Iraqi friends. I must admit I was always glad when they got back safely.

The temperature was usually in the 90s and we devised water games in the garden, playing with a hose and all the watering cans and buckets. The roof being flat was an obvious vantage point, and our games were very childish. Once my shirt got torn to shreds, so they tied the shreds to the rose bushes in the garden. Next time in, they bought me a special new shirt that would not tear. In fact, it was made of nail cloth and when I got into it, I couldn't get my arms down.

There was also good shooting near Basra, and I was able to take parties of Naval officers after snipe or duck when they could come. These small sloops were very hot, and it was a happy change for them to get ashore. We were lucky really, as almost exactly opposite our house was the club, with a swimming pool and tennis courts.

The airport at that time was only a drawing and the work of levelling the aerodrome had begun, with donkeys removing the earth in their twin baskets. I suppose about twenty or thirty men were employed at levelling this vast area. Now staying with the topic of transport, I think there was only one train up to Baghdad each day and one down, as well as a few goods trains. The distance was about 350 miles and I felt I knew every milepost, having worked in the two divisions for so long. I was most anxious to get more experience, and while Basra was a lot of fun, it was awfully hot and (as far as I could see) there was no chance of a bridge project there. In the meantime, my former work colleague Brigadier General M.G. Lubbock, who had been in Baghdad when I first joined the railway, and had long since retired to England, was on the board of the Sao Paulo railway. That railway needed a Chief Engineer, and the post was offered to M.G. Lubbock. So M.G. resigned and after fifteen years in that hot climate he and Mrs. Lubbock left Iraq and returned to England to make the journey to Brazil. To our great sorrow while in London Mrs. Lubbock died and he had to go off to South America alone.

About a year after this Lubbock wrote and asked me to join him as Bridge Engineer to the Sao Paulo Railway. Of course, it was a marvellous offer and I accepted at once. I suppose with all big changes in our life, we have mixed feelings. Leaving Iraq was tough, as we had so many friends still living there. Colonel Tainah was not in favour of our leaving and even came to Basra to tell me I was making a mistake. I was very sorry to leave them. Also, my friend Brough Sadler and his wife were still in Baghdad, but I think they were on leave when I had to make the decision. I generally went to Brough with my problems, as he was always kind and understanding.

We heard that Brazil was a beautiful country, and the climate was certainly better than Iraq. There would be a very busy railway with masses of engineering to be done, bridges, tunnels and viaducts. I could not resist any of this. Even in those days the move was half-way around the world, and we had most of our worldly possessions with us. Many decisions had to be made, such as forwarding our boxes and cases straight to Brazil, as we went on three months leave in England and Ireland.

Goodbyes are always painful, but none more so than to Miritch, the bearer I had had almost all the time I was in Iraq. There were many others also among my Arab friends, like Anfus who looked after the horses, and Awar and Kescor, brothers who worked with me on the railway line; trolly-men on the book, but in reality, they kept me in touch with all railway matters, and were willing to guard me with their lives if needs be. For example, during one hot summer when I was at Diwaniyah, there was some trouble brewing at Rumaitha and I got a message that I should go down and sort things out. I was not too happy about this, as it was not so very long after the rebellion which I had been very much involved in back then. I made ready to leave by motor trolley. Things were so tense that I'd even written a letter to my wife – who was in England at the time – in case I was shot. Anyway, when I went out to the motor trolley, there were all my staff, armed and ready to come with me. As it turned out, there was no chance of any harm coming to me with this lot, many of whom belonged to the tribe that I was to deal with.

We eventually departed Iraq in 1935. In my mind's eye, I can still see some of the Arabs I had known for so long running after the train to wish us *'God Speed'*, saying *"Go with God, Allah Akbah!"*

Chapter 10

Appointed Bridge Engineer for the Sao Paulo Railways

We sailed on the Arcturus 1st class to Brazil. This was a most luxurious cruise and we reached Santos three weeks later having visited Lisbon, Madeira and Rio de Janeiro on the way. All were most beautiful places, but especially so after years in the desert. Pre-war luxury liners were an experience never to be forgotten, marvellous food, seven course dinners and with everything imaginable *'there for the asking.'*

Brazilian ladies seemed to be among the best dressed in the world, and most of those we met on the voyage were returning from London and Paris, where no doubt they'd bought a few dresses. In fact, we never saw the same dress twice and they changed three to four times a day. I could see this was going to be very different from Iraq. Also, M.G. (Bill) Lubbock was with us on the voyage, and we enjoyed it all. As we neared Brazil, we sensed that Bill (as we now called him) was not too happy, maybe because of what he had asked us to do. This wasn't helped by the sudden change in the value of Brazilian currency, which overnight reduced my salary by half against the pound sterling. In the meantime, we were studying

Portuguese, since we knew we'd have to speak it, as no English was spoken in the shops or on the telephone, and there were no English newspapers.

Rio was of course quite beautiful, blue sea surrounding dozens of little islands, a white surf breaking on the rocks, trees everywhere in flower, and miles of beaches and soft warm air. Santos too was very pretty in a much more quaint and smaller way, and from here the train went up to the Alto de Serra, which was 3000 feet up and beautiful when the sun shone. But sadly, it was often enveloped in mist, with mildew growing overnight and the flowers consequently hidden sometimes for weeks on end.

When we first arrived in Brazil, we stayed with Bill in his house called a 'chacara'. It was a nice little one-story house with a woodland garden and a riding school. By now he had two English thoroughbreds which he rode and schooled for jumping (this he did loose over the fences). He also had a retired English jockey as a groom, and we had a lot of fun.

We slept in an extraordinary room over the garage, with a ladder down to the bathroom. Early on we went to inspect the place that I was to be sent, and I had to choose between two houses which were vacant. They were both railway houses and seemed to have been painted inside and out with the usual brown paint, which most stations were painted with in those days. Very soon after that we were invited to meet the Wellingtons. Mr. Wellington was the superintendent of the railway, and their house was not far from where we were staying with Bill. They had made a beautiful garden with lawns and trees, a swimming pool, as well as roses and all sorts of

English flowers (including some of the best dahlias I have ever seen).

We met their dogs and admired their horses, and came to know them very well, learning a great deal about South America and other things. They were always most awfully kind. I used to think how lucky the S.P.R. was to have a fellow like Alec Wellington who understood the Brazilians so well and could speak their language perfectly, which was not an easy assignment with so many different nationalities.

Each day something happened that made us realise that everything was going to be absolutely different from Iraq. We had left the quiet dignity of the East and here was the garish noisy West. Even in expensive hotels and restaurants a frightful game was played with dice, where each player dashed the dice on to the table with great speed; not one, but three or more large dice, with all sorts of calls and scores. If I remember correctly, this game was called Bidoo and although it was perhaps great fun, my own personal opinion at the time was that the playing of it should be restricted to a padded cell!

In addition, the dignity and hospitality of the Arabs as compared with the indifference of the Brazilian was very noticeable, until one remembers they are mostly exiles. The poor indigenous Brazilian will always offer his food, his seat, or his house. The population is composed of people from all over Europe and from Japan. Jews of German nationality were pouring in to escape Hitler, and many very distinguished Jews made a new home in Brazil.

At that time there was a tremendous feeling of upheaval, and the abdication of Edward VIII astounded the country. Strangers would ask about it in the train or in the street: *"Can it be true that England will let her King go because of a woman?"* The newspapers even had extra additions and huge headlines, since as a prince, Edward had visited Brazil.

Chapter 11

Bridge construction, experiment in diving, and dealing with a 40-foot mud swamp

My job in Brazil was very interesting, since there were several bridges to build, strengthen and repair. In fact, there were no less than 27 bridges and 13 tunnels on the inclines from the Alto da Serra to Santos. It's also worth noting that this was a cable railway with standing engines, with eight trains moving simultaneously every eight minutes, four up and four down (with each made up of two or three coaches). A far cry from Iraq! During one year at the Alto da Serra while we lived there, rain fell every day. In contrast, while we were at Diwaniyah in Iraq there was one year when not one drop of rain fell!

We lived on the top of a steep hill with a winding footpath, with many steps and no driveway. The conventional two-storied house was made of wood and was very well built, with beautiful, polished floors and shuttered windows. There was a veranda on two sides, and an enormous magnolia tree near the hall door. When we had thunder, the lightning would run down the wet leaves of the magnolia with a loud cracking noise.

Inside one forgot that it was a wooden house, as all the panelling was painted a very pale green. The bedrooms looked out over the hills and flowering forest, and there was almost always something in flower, such as tibushina, which is called "yesterday, today and tomorrow" (because the flowers change colour from white to mauve to magenta). Near the window there was a huge buddleia often covered with many different butterflies, and the smell of orange blossom was also never far away. In addition, the abundance of timber was extraordinary, and the house was heated by the timber burned in open fires in every room, and all the cooking was done with wood.

In Iraq we had only men servants, whereas in Brazil we had women, including Portuguese, Spanish, Polish and Italian, as well as one coloured indigenous woman whose little family lived nearby in a tiny shack on the hill. Believe it or not, six of these girls got married while they were with us, and after each left, we always had difficulty getting another.

There was a profusion of lovely fruit, figs, strawberries, avocados and mangoes, as well as many we had not seen before. Also, there always seemed to be the smell of coffee in the air.

In 1931 when I visited Professor Wooley at Ur of the Chaldees, he showed me a roof timber truss which they had taken from some excavation at Ur. He said it had been there for about 5000 years, and it was still as good as the day the house was built because it had never been wet. I've a theory that if timber is kept absolutely dry or fully immersed in water it will last forever. However, in Brazil there was little chance of wood surviving long. This was because Brazil is home to insects called Torede or Limeria, which eat through timber at great speed. For example, during the construction of the Piasaguera bridge, we had a temporary diversion. It was in use for about two years, and we used to allow the trains to travel at 40 m.p.h. on it. In this diversion the piles were initially 12 by 12-inch timber with a forty-foot penetration. However, when the work was finished and we removed these piles, they had reduced to 6 by 6 inches. We were amazed that the Torede could have eaten so much so quickly. These creatures leave a small white mark and bore like mad.

The foot bridge at the Alto da Serra had been there since about 1900 and there were no completion plans to be found. Since the over-head had to be raised, I thought it might be well to see what it was resting on. I was astonished to find that when one of the piers was opened up, this foot bridge was actually standing on square holes 30 feet deep. There was not a scrap of wood left. In this case the cause was one of the dry rot family. To rectify the problem, we filled the holes with concrete and regarded them as piles.

In the dense places the virgin jungle could be quite dark, and usually there are little drops of water from the trees. Everyone carried a knife. There was often a fear of getting lost and snakes were dangerous, though I seldom saw one. There were also beautiful orchids growing, but they were usually too high up to cut.

I played a certain amount of polo in Brazil. Now in those days the Brazilians were still learning to play as a team, as they are the great individualists. It was often difficult to umpire strictly, and on one occasion when I was an arbitrator, they said that if I blew the whistle once more that, *"They would all go off the field."* So, one of our Brazilian friends who was an excellent umpire, when I asked him why was it that I had so much difficulty umpiring, and yet he got instant obedience, he replied, *"I carry an automatic!"*

Playing polo in Brazil

Firearms were easy to come by, and one of the many tragedies that occurred during our stint in Brazil was the murder of a tall good-looking Englishman called 'Bachelor'. He was employed on Vesty's citrus and banana plantation at San Sebastian. We had stayed there for a polo match and later Bachelor and his wife had stayed with us on their honeymoon. About one week later when Bachelor (who was one of the managers) was walking around the banana lines, he noticed that one of the men was not using the special knife provided. He said to the man, *"You must use the right knife."* He may have had to say it before. San Sebastian was on the coast, and it is very humid in these fruit farms. As a result, tempers could run hot rather quickly. The man objected and then he went away to a bar and drank several small pingas. This spirit is made from raw sugar cane and is very potent, and in those days it was very cheap. Afterwards, instead of getting the knife to cut the bananas, this man went along to near Bachelor's house and waited. When Bachelor came out, he shot him dead. He then disappeared into the jungle for a time, but he was eventually caught and tried, and then sentenced to six months in gaol.

Staying with the topic of troublemakers, I had a man at the Alto da Serra giving a lot of trouble. He would get drunk and frighten people. I said he must be moved to the bottom of the 'inclines', since this was thought of as punishment, as it was very much hotter than in the Alto. He refused to move and continued to be a nuisance, even threatening to shoot me and my assistant Stuart Mc Neill. I then wrote to the Sao Paulo office warning them that if he did attempt to shoot me, then I would shoot him first. The tension was heightened by the fact that we were having continuous mist at the time, and it was difficult to see who was coming out of the mist; so everyone was anxious about this, as he was still about the place.

When my letter was received, the Superintendent telephoned to warn me, saying, *"Do you know that you will get 23 years in gaol if you shoot this man?"*

I replied that Bachelor's murderer only got six months.

His response was, *"But he was a Brazilian."*

And that was the disparity of justice in Brazil at the time!

I did not know many Irishmen in Brazil but there were one or two outstanding people, one of whom was Russell Warren the principal doctor in Sao Paulo. I think he was a surgeon but the only professional job he did for me was cutting out some ticks after my trip to the Matte Grosse. He was an old Trinity College Dublin man, and he was very highly thought of. On one of our visits to the Warrens, Russell told me of the gold mine he had found. He was terribly keen on this and said to me, *"You must come in on this as it is going to be really important."* He then produced a little bit of quartz, white quartz I think, and it showed little specks of gold and looked awfully easy. I said to him, *"Is it going to be very expensive to get this gold out?"* He replied, *"No I don't think it is, but you must come and see what you think."* So, it was all arranged that we would go to the borders of the Matte Grosse. I don't remember how far it was, but three of us started off in this car. We had terrific rains and the car got stuck and we spent hours digging ourselves out; all of which was lucky for me because we never got to this gold mine of his. I think he put a fair amount of money into this project, but whether he ever got anything out of it I do not know. I do know that there is a gold mine which is one of the deepest in the world owned by de Beers and that they make perhaps 10% on their money.

I had another Irish friend in Santos who was a sort of coffee king. He bought most of the coffee for the U.S., and we often had lunch together and he was full of fun. The doctor had told him that to keep fit he should ride a horse every day, as he was having too many good dinners and needed exercise. So 'Mul' bought three horses and one day he asked me to come along the beach with him, to try out one of his horses. There were various parties bathing and sunbathing, and Mul seemed to know them all and called out greetings and swept off his hat. Similarly, I tried to do polite things with my hat. After some time and lots of greetings, Mul complained that I was taking off my hat to all the wrong women. With this I quickly realised that I'd never in a million years learn the hand shaking and hat removing etiquette of Brazil – it was all so complicated! Also, I think Mul may have invented some of the so-called etiquette rules for himself. Anyway, that day I went along to his very nice house, where I was shown his reversible paintings, which were cathedrals on one side and lovely girls on the other. He told me that a lot of his friends were priests who came from the Matto Grosse to visit him, and seeing the cathedrals they were very impressed. But one time they arrived without warning and found his lovely girls in the frames, so they were not amused. However, I suspect Mul had a good laugh.

Now one of the greatest problems in Brazil was the heavy rainfall, with an average of about 150 inches a year. On the Serra this caused 'slips', and the railway could become unworkable. One of my first jobs at the Alto da Serra was to try and find out where the underground streams came from, and then drain them away before they did damage. We employed a water diviner to help, but he showed so many streams that often, from a tunnelling point of view, it was impossible to check his findings.

There was one very difficult case above a deep ravine called 'Grotto Fundo', where quite a large hill was moving slowly towards viaduct 16 and the railway tunnel beside it. To try fix the problem, we laid on a 4-foot pipe and connected it to a stream, which was about 100 feet above; and with this powerful water jet, we cut a valley between the hill, the tunnel and viaduct below. During this procedure, there was always the danger of boulders sweeping down. We had one boulder of between 300 to 400 tons, and these large ones had to be broken up by hand. This was because it was too dangerous to use explosives in case of causing fractures which might open up later. The work on the boulders was done very cleverly by Italian stone masons, who used pointed pegs followed by square pegs which they called pinheiros and pinchotis. When these were driven in skillfully, the rock would split for 15 or 20 feet.

There were some very difficult bridges to build between Santos and the bottom of the Serra. The largest was near to Santos and across the Casqueiro river. Actually, this largest bridge was in fact two bridges, with each laid with single track and having three 186-foot spans. The river here was very tidal, and the first twenty or thirty feet was of liquid mud, so that the caissons had to be suspended on steel strips; and these were attached to a timber piled framework around the caissons. Needless to say, here our instrument work had to be extremely accurate.

In this job I unfortunately had some difficulties with the contractor, an English firm who were not as careful as I was. When it came to plugging the caissons which they had brought out to Brazil, the bottom-hanging-boxes that they had, had already been used on a bridge on the Zambesi. Since the wells in that African bridge were a different shape, these boxes would not open properly, and this meant that they would not deposit concrete at the plug. Because it would be a mixture mostly of gravel, I could not allow this. As a result, they were very angry and cabled that I should be removed. I had already had trouble with the same firm about rivets. I said that the rivets had been caulked and had them cut out.

At Cubatao bridge we were putting in 4-foot diameter screw piles and here we had another English firm, who were doing an excellent job. However, instead of the screw piles at each end, it was thought we might economize if we put in spread abutments. So, I wrote to the Chief Engineer pointing out that I had taken a trial shaft and that it showed a line of silt running in above the bed of the river and near to these abutments. I thought it would be dangerous and he agreed with me and wrote as much to the consultants. They did not agree and told us to get on with the job.

We put in these spread abutments, each of about 500 tons of reinforced concrete, and as soon as the bridge was opened to traffic, both abutments began to sink, and we had to revert to the old line. The approach from the north was over swamp countryside (of about 40 feet of liquid mud for a mile), so we had to realign the track. To do this we decided to make a mattress of trees, which we hauled from a nearby forest with mules. About ten thousand trees were placed and tied with sepe creeper, which grows in these forests and is used for rope. Instead of the spread abutments we drove piles with an 80-foot penetration. To do this we used a 5-ton drop-hammer. The drop was 12 feet and the pile measured 18 by 18 inches. On these piles we were able to build our abutments. I think it is interesting that within a year we were able to run the trains at 50 or 60 miles per hour over this swamp.

The hydro-electric scheme on the top of these hills was not far from Cubatao. It comprised lakes being joined together on the plateau 3000 feet above our railway (which runs through to Santos). At this point they had a drop of 2000 feet, so this was a brilliant energy-producing idea for the scheme. An American named Mr Billings was the engineer who'd built it. I met Billings shortly after I arrived in Brazil, and he told me some of the problems of the swamp, such as how in one case a bridge had disappeared completely on them. He said that an inexperienced engineer had had a supposed 'brainwave'. To get added strength he had encased the steel in concrete, without considering the enormous added weight on the foundations. The swamp gobbled his brainwave up!

Near to Piasageura there was another bridge being built with open caisson construction, and we were having great difficulty in lowering the caisson. We had gone through boulders and stones, and I felt I had better go down and see if I could find out what was holding it up. So, they let me down in a bucket and I warned them, *"If it sinks suddenly, for heaven's sake, pull me up."* When I got down, I could see nothing that could be stopping the cutting edge of the caisson. But then quite suddenly I realised how stupid I had been, because obviously the outside friction of the boulders against the caisson was the cause. I shouted to them to put water on the outside, and this had an immediate effect and the caisson started to move. At this stage I was very frightened and called out, *"Pull me up quickly before I'm buried alive!"*

At another bridge a diver had been employed for years to go down and inspect the piers or cylinders, and if he found hair cracks, he would place steel bands around the cylinders. I thought it might be interesting to see what was really going on down there, so I got into his outfit, and they lowered me down about 40 feet. Down that deep I couldn't actually see anything. When I asked the diver what he had seen, he replied that he'd seen nothing either. After that we had a powerful Lukas lamp fitted on his helmet. By the way, diving is a very frightening employment.

One very odd thing about living at the Alto da Serra and going up and down the mountain was that it was much more exhausting than one would think. While at the top we were often enveloped in mist: in contrast at the same time down below it might be very hot sunshine. Before breakfast I often walked out to look at various works that were going on, would return back to breakfast absolutely drenched, and would eventually end up having to change completely. Working down the inclines, this would be hot and sticky with high humidity. If I meant to stay down, then I would have to change again, and so on, since it was quite dangerous to go up in wet clothes.

All this was very tiresome, and one fell asleep rather easily. I remember how once a party was arranged for our consultants who had come out from London. Anyway, after one of these long days of inspection we all met at a hotel in Sao Paulo. We were determined to entertain these distinguished visitors and Mr. Wellington was telling thrilling tales of thunder and lightning, with balls of blue flame running down the trees and around the golf course. But in the meantime, Mr. Lubbock, sitting beside one of the visitors had fallen asleep. When out of the blue he was suddenly asked if he had experienced these awful thunderstorms, he feigned wakefulness, blinked a bit and said, *"Nonsense, we don't have thunder here!"*

Once I went to one of those parties after having been to the occultist, when I must have been quite blinded by the drops he had put in my eyes. Anyway, I did not realise it until I tried to pay the taxi, and almost as soon as I got into the room a waiter handed me a huge dish of cocktail 'eats'. I was a little surprised and I wanted to get rid of it, so I saw a table not far off, and intending to lay my dish down on it, instead I mistakenly dropped the whole thing on the carpet. All the guests had been waiting for these rather splendid eats for ages, and my stupidity meant nobody would enjoy them that day.

There was a most persuasive type of fellow that I had met once or twice, and he seemed to get away with all sorts of fraud. I should say that the taxi drivers in Brazil were not celebrated for their kindliness, but this fellow was such a good fraudster that he managed to borrow money from several of them in Sao Paulo. He had a job helping on a farm where there were a lot of Japanese working, and the farmer had arranged a theatrical entertainment of some sort to amuse these workers. However, the farmer was disappointed that they did not seem very pleased about it. Sometime later he found out that his helper had not only made them pay to get in, but he also made them pay to get out as well.

We had a new Consul General in Sao Paulo. He left Germany on one of the last trains out of that unhappy country, and it was laden with the refugees he had helped to get away. He arrived in Brazil with his lovely blond wife and daughter. His wife was Norwegian, and they owned a tiny island off the Dalmatian coast. Although every corner of their lives seemed to be shattered, because they had so much intimate knowledge of the sufferings caused by Hitler's pogroms, their own distress was hardly mentioned. In a strange way this little family represented the heroism and charm of the pre-war era and represented (for me at least) the epitome of the world ruined by the Fascists. I think that the Consul for England had great influence in Brazil joining the Allies, as there had been a good deal of uncertainty in the lead-up to the war, a war that turned all our lives upside down!

Chapter 12

Battle of the River Plate, and myself the 'Hangman from Africa'

The Second World War lasted from 1939 to 1945. During the war the battle of the River Plate was fought when we were still in Brazil. Just before the war erupted in September 1939, H.M.S. Exeter had visited Santos and we had met some of its officers. Also, they visited us at the Alto and rode our horses, and the wife of the Commander of Dragon came and stayed with us. When a direct hit was made on the gun turret of the Exeter killing several people, among them a Lieutenant Bowman Mannifold (who had so recently ridden our horses), we felt very sad indeed for the loss of this splendid young officer.

There were many wild stories about the battle. One which I have not heard contradicted was quite interesting. It was said that when divers went down in the vicinity of the Graf Spee – the German battleship scuttled by Captain Langsdorff at the mouth of the River Plate – they found that there were bodies in the battleship. This set up a line of enquiry and the coffins which had been carried with so much solemnity to a most enormous funeral and attended by many nation's representatives, were in fact packed with rifles and ammunition – an instalment of supplies for a revolution which would take over Uruguay for Hitler.

Early in the war things were very tricky, as we had Germans and Italians on the staff of the Sao Paulo Railways, and they were not all nationalised Brazilians. I wondered if I should carry a revolver, but was told that as I certainly could not use it, there would not be much point.

I remember that about this period we had about 40 men whose job was to clean steel for painting, and they did not seem to me to work very hard. As we had 10,000 tons of steel it was very important. For this reason, I got into a boiler suit and went down to where they were working and worked with them for a day or two. I soon discovered that these fellows were really doing only about one hour a day, so I said that if they did not work, they would all be suspended. The very next day the Santos newspaper had an article about the 'Hangman' who had come from Africa. This was my good self! As it turned out, later on they all worked very well; and since it really was a filthy job, I was able to get them more pay.

Beg (referred to previously as the Irish doctor with the gold mine) had many strange stories to tell. One was about P.C. Scherpenberg, who had come to Brazil in search of land suitable for Dutch settlement. I think he had ridden over thousands of miles exploring the interior as it is called. Another of Beg's stories I remember was about a place where people from all over Europe were looking for diamonds; they stood either in the river or near the edge, filling and emptying a sort of pan and watching the sand flow out. They did this for days and weeks and even months on end, in the hope of finding a diamond which would make them rich.

Usually in such remote places there was a bar and a dance floor where they spent their evenings. These places were constructed with timber and branches and were in no way permanent. When a fight occurred, the police would quickly push their rifles through the lattice and rake the dance floor with bullets. This scheme put an end to many arguments, as well as perhaps the odd life!

Chapter 13

Ten days in the Matto Grosse, alligators, piranha and others

I was due for some local leave, and we had often talked of going to the Matto Grosso in search of wild pig. By now Beg knew this very difficult country better than most people. He told us about the Grand Pantanal, where the Rio Paraguay forms the border with Bolivia. He said that this country was teeming with wildlife and that it was a lovely country to ride over. The small river which waters this part is the Rio Negro. It dries up in summertime, except for pools where the alligators collect.

We travelled up in a railway saloon through the state of Sao Paulo and through the Matte Grosso, as far as the Bolivian border. This meant changing to two other railway systems, altogether about 1500 kms. The rail journey involved three days travel through woodland. There was very little grassland as we know it, it was rather hot, and the coach was full of flying creatures. Porto Esperanca was the Rail Head station and arriving at it, we left the train and there was Beg with 24 horses and about 6 men. He also had an ox-wagon, which he said we would need to carry anyone who did not want to ride, as well as the camp kit and barrels of water (as we could not depend on the river).

Syracio was the head man. He was a dark-skinned indigenous Indian, a beautiful horseman and spoke with a quiet dignity. He could tell the signs of wind and weather. Most of the men carried revolvers and they all carried knives, big facao stuck into their belts.

The ponies were clean and in good condition. Though I am sure they had never seen a brush, they were beautifully trained and stood still while we mounted; even with our own saddles, which were quite different from the saddles they were accustomed to. These horses are taught to neck rein, which is a very easy way of directing the animal by just holding the reins to right or left so that the neck of the animal feels the light pressure.

In order to plan this trip, Beg had ridden a distance of about 250 kms in the three days before we arrived. He offered 1000 pounds if we saw another human being before we got back. We were amazed, but in fact his money was safe. We would ride in a northerly direction aiming at the Rio Miranda, where indeed he had organised a boat to meet us for fishing. The country was a luscious meadowland, and the air was full of bird noises, parrots and macaws, as well as many strangers, tiny red birds and also birds that looked like very thin hens. The parrots screamed at us as they flew from tree to tree. In addition, we saw duck in the air or on land, but never down on the water, as the alligators were so plentiful that a duck would be swallowed instantly.

Our first camp was a krall called a 'retiro' or place where cattle are rounded up from time to time. But here there was no water, so we had to use the water from the barrels we had brought with us. Our next camp was near a pool not any larger than a tennis court, and (believe it or not) I actually counted 27 alligators in it! The water looked clean enough when it had settled, so we boiled it and the horses drank with a loud sucking noise as if they were straining it. We had not thought about water being a problem, as there seemed to be so many rivers, but one morning I heard Bill solemnly say, *"Dash it all, I have drunk the water I'd meant to shave with."*

I slept in a camp bed, but some of the party slept in hammocks, which meant that two trees had to be found which were the right distance apart. When the trees had been found, then one had to be sure that there was not a trail of ants leading into the hammock. Some people had to find another tree in the middle of the night, and as the hammocks had mosquito nets fixed inside, getting in and out of bed was a bit of a struggle.

We came to one place where there were so many alligators that it looked as if the whole bank of the river was slipping into the water. Sometimes they would sit up and bark at us or at each other. Once I remember Syracio threw his lasso and caught one of these creatures, as I tried to photograph it. But it was too dangerous to go near, and the photograph wasn't very clear.

There were also some beautiful deer, one was as tall as a horse, light reddish fawn with black ear tips. Unfortunately, the camera was rarely to hand when we needed to snap such wild animals in their natural habitat.

Most days we rode for about 8 hours, but on this last day we roused ourselves at 4 am. This was so that the oxen could travel in the cool of day, as we were very uncertain of the distance to the Rio Miranda, and we had to be sure of getting there for water. By midday the oxen had lain down, so we ate our picnic and rested for an hour or so. The temperature was about 100 degrees Fahrenheit and there were thousands of mosquitos. We drank masses of tea and water with lemon squeezed in (since we still had a few lemons).

Beg and Syracio rode off to see where the river lay, and when they came back, they said they had seen a line of trees, and it would be no distance. We started off again at 3.30 pm, and although we rode in a direct line and passed several lines of trees, it was 7.30 pm before we reached the river. By now it was quite dark, a lovely night, with the sky full of stars. Even though it was rather eerie, the horses cantered along seeming to enjoy the cool air.

The onca-Brazilian jaguar was greatly feared, and there was always a chance of a snake, who would make your horse stop so suddenly that it was hard not to fall off. We were told there could even be puma (the so-called American lion), but we didn't see them. We lit a big fire to direct the ox-wagon and to keep off mosquitos, and when the wagon arrived, we cooked a meal, fixed our beds and hammocks, and thankfully went to sleep.

The river where we would have liked to have bathed and fished was very disappointing. It was full of the dreaded piranha, and we had to be careful even filling a bucket. In addition, we were all very black, as the country gets burned every year by forest fires, which start up perhaps hundreds of miles away and spread with the wind (leaving the ground black, while the vegetation looks healthy and succulent). Sometimes whole trees were lifted up in flames.

The canoe had arrived and with it were two men who knew all about fishing. They said that there were dorado in the river which would be very good to eat. However, there were also piranha, and it would be hard not to catch them, as they would take any bait. Alec was the only fisherman amongst us, and in fact he tried very hard, but after several catches – always a piranha – he made bets he could catch six piranhas in five minutes without losing a finger. He did this, but most of the time was spent in getting the fish off the hook. They are the most extraordinary fish, only about 12 inches long and with huge strong mouths and a passionate desire for flesh.

After a trial with various bait and always the same result, Alec next said that he would catch his piranha with a piece of his shirt. So, we watched him solemnly cut a piece off his shirt, fold it into a neat bait and then put it on the hook. The piranhas weren't interested, and he lost his bet.

We stayed in this camp for three days resting, as well as attempting to wash our shirts. We would gladly have thrown them into the river if we had not needed them again on the way home. However, one or two shirts did eventually go to the fish. The horses too were glad of the rest, although they just followed along when they were not being ridden; as we each had four horses and only changed over whenever we thought they were getting tired.

While camping, several varieties of ants gave us a lot of bother, as they got into our beds, clothes, shoes and food. The ants in Brazil make a huge anthill where they lay their eggs. These hills are treacherous to ride near and sometimes the ground is soft with deep holes. Indeed, one or two of our group fell heavily because the horse had put his foot near an anthill.

On the last day we made a straight line on the map, cutting off a corner, as we had to get to the train. It turned out to be the longest day of all. We left camp at 4.30 am, having packed up all the filthy clothes and (by now) filthy food, and we were all looking forward to our railway coach with its comparative luxury. We had not been riding for long when we saw a most beautiful anteater called Tomandua Bandeira. This animal was over 3 feet at the shoulder, her tail nearly as long as her body, and a little arm seemed to be holding on to it. It was only when we got near enough, we could see that a miniature of herself was lying across her back, with the same black and white markings and the same long snout. These animals are almost holy because they eat the ant larva, putting their long noses into the ant hills. Hence the old maxim: *"Kill the ant or the ant will kill Brazil!"*

After we had been riding for some hours through rather nice meadow land, there were signs of pig rootings, so we let Beg go through a little wood with some of the party while the rest of us waited. Presently, out of the wood came dozens of little pigs of all sizes, ages and sexes. There must have been about 200 altogether, sleek and shiny and the little ones looking like tabby cats.

Syracio on his beautiful white mare chased after a boar, holding his spear high in stabbing fashion, and on his own he killed this animal in one stroke. We realised that this was not the sport we had been looking for, and decided that these pigs were too small, even though they ran like mad and put up a good fight. Following this, we went our way and with one or two stops we reached the train at 7 pm.

Here indeed was nature conserved in all its splendour, and looking back, it's hard to see where man fits in: especially when one has battled thousands of mosquitos, flies and ants and there are about a dozen ticks a day on various parts of one's body (indeed I had to have mine cut out in hospital in Sao Paulo); or when the danger of snakes or scorpions makes it unsafe to step out of bed in the dark; or when a fire has to be kept lighting to frighten away the larger animals; or when the most dangerous spider in the world – for which there is no serum – has been seen in the afternoon; or when little fish called piranhas are waiting to devour a leg or an arm. No, it is not hard for the most humane of humans to beat off this multitude of nature's onslaughts with a certain satisfaction; the marvel is that man has ever ventured into these places and survived.

Our last year in Brazil was far from happy. I had written to the war office to ask if they wanted me, and Bill was not too pleased about this. He seemed to think that in some way I was letting him down. Bill was ten years older than me, and I expect he wanted to go himself, but there was little hope of that. Either ways, they replied to me that if I were in England there was no doubt that I could be of use, but that at my age they could not offer me anything definite.

At this juncture in the war, Brazil had not yet taken sides, and it was a very uncomfortable feeling. When I consequently resigned from the Sao Paulo Railway, this didn't suit them at all. They had no wish to pay my six-year pension fund, nor my fare to England, nor the leave pay which was now due to me. I won only two of these battles and the pension fund (to which I contributed regularly), was never paid.

In order to leave Brazil, one had to have a visa to return, even if you assured the authorities that you had no wish to return; except perhaps as a tourist to admire their beautiful coastline. Visas have stamps – I cannot remember the value – and in order to get these stamps I had to employ an agent. I think I was charged £50 for my wife and myself, for about seven stamps. This whole performance was a lot more costly (and nearly as painful) as the process of obtaining a driver's license for my wife about two years before. Again, she had to have an 'agent' and also travel to a station halfway to Sao Paulo, leaving at seven o' clock in the morning to wait in a long line (alongside many suspected criminals) at a police station. It was a similar long wait for her later at the doctor's (even though there seemed to be no patients), so that she could undergo a test that is called a bill of 'sanidade' (which sounds like 'sanity'). This test is necessary to have to get one's license. Hard to believe but after all these bureaucratic hurdles, my wife didn't have to do an actual driving test itself to get her license. Eventually, we all felt utmost relief when she got a nice-little amateurs driving licence with stamps to the value of 15/-. The cost was £7.10, and even then, I had to compensate the agent.

Bidding farewell to Brazil in the early days of the Second World War, before the United States joined it in 1941, we said 'goodbye' to our friends after a series of farewell parties and travelled on a neutral American liner to New Orleans.

Chapter 14

Leaving Brazil and travels to New Orleans, Toronto, Montreal, Liverpool and Dublin (1941)

On that journey Beg and his wife and baby travelled with us. He was coming home to join the Free Dutch Army and at that time they were training in Canada. As I mentioned, the U.S. was not yet at war so we travelled with lights on and in comparative luxury – one day at Rio, then a stop at Pernambuco, and then the Caribbean. It was in the Caribbean that we heard an American ship had been sunk, and we subsequently picked up some of their survivors. I think about eight men had already been rescued by some other ship.

When we reached the Mississippi, it wasn't long before we arrived into New Orleans, where the peace of our luxury liner was suddenly dashed by a hoard of newspaper men, who had come to question the survivors. It was my first experience of U.S. reporters. They occupied our chairs and tables and pushed us about on deck. As a result, most of us retired to our cabins and missed seeing this historic landscape.

Later we disembarked into New Orleans with its lovely French architecture and happy people, and it all seemed very peaceful. We planned to travel by Greyhound coach and went off to find a hotel, where we stayed for a night. In the meantime, all our heavy baggage went ahead to Toronto, where it remained until the war was over. By the way, I forgot to mention earlier, that during our last few weeks in Brazil we'd sold all our furniture and most of our belongings, so we only had a 'bare minimum'. This so-called 'bare minimum' (according to my wife) was contained in no less than 17 cases, all of which were weighed, measured and counted over and over again! How we ended up with so many cases was because my wife insisted on bringing home our most prized belongings. A perfect example of one such belonging was a picture she fell in love with in Brazil. Seeing it one day while out shopping, she walked up and down in front of the shop window until we decided to buy it. Although I felt very foolish for bringing it all the way back to Europe, nevertheless we still have it to this day, and it's a painting which everyone still admires.

But getting back to New Orleans, one day my wife and Mildred van Scherpenberg were walking along with a baby carriage holding Katherine (who was then 6 months old). To their astonishment a gentleman passerby stopped and politely asked, *"Say Mam, is that a Norwegian baby?"* Mildred replied, *"No, she is Brazilian."* To this the American said, *"Well she is just like all those lovely babies in Norway."* Mildred had to admit that she was a Norwegian herself, so, the man was very discerning.

It was the end of June and very warm in the Southern states, the greyhound coach was airconditioned and the journey up through the United States to Canada took five or six days. My most distinct recollection is perpetually yearning for something to drink, since it was hot! Each time the coach stopped for the day, we left it to stay at a hotel. As I remember the different states had different drinking laws. In some places to get a drink we had to sit at a table and pay for a plate full of dry sandwiches, which went from table to table and were never eaten. Then at other places one was not allowed to sit down in the bar. I remember we reached Atlanta city on a Sunday and the only way to get a drink there was to have it sent to the hotel bedroom. Also, you had to order a whole bottle, and as you could not carry it in public, this meant you either had to finish it or leave it. To an Irishman and a Dutchman coming from Brazil, all these drinking restrictions were like a red rag to a bull, and enough to start a terrible thirst!

After travelling up the U.S. by Greyhound, we next visited Toronto, Canada, where we stayed with my sister for about ten days and ate the most beautiful food. In Toronto, drink could only be bought at an 'off-licence' and 'no lady could enter'. My Canadian brother-in-law was horrified when my wife attempted to collect some bottles of ale. While at my sister's, she had filled her refrigerator with meat and all sorts of goodies like raspberries, strawberries and cream – which we really relished. This was especially so, as we knew we'd soon be returning to the strict rationing of war-engulfed England. So, every bite was savoured as though it were our last.

Also, while in Canada, we were taken to the Country Club and here again there was a shadow over drink. I distinctly recall my host giving me a sherry out of his locker in the gentlemen's room, with as much guilt as if we were smoking in the school dormitory.

We sailed from Quebec in a Free French ship, which had been in battle and had several scars. There were only 8 passengers and in one of those odd coincidences, one of these was the sister of an old friend in Iraq. They were coming home from Hong Kong and had come across Canada. We had a lot to talk about.

This ship had a French crew and Chinese stewards. We asked when we would meet our convoy and were told there would be no convoy as they could do only 16 knots max. I lent the captain my binoculars, as he had lost his in one of the battles. Thankfully, we did not see any submarines; but as we dropped depth charges and saw enormous splashes, we at last began to feel we were in the war. Coming through a smooth blue sea where H.M.S. Hood had so recently been lost made it all seem very near.

Arriving eventually in Liverpool, there was nothing sentimental about it, only the customs ransacking our baggage piece by piece, and air raid sirens going off as soon as we were in bed. By now English cities were being pulverised by the Luftwaffe. Surviving some of those bombs in Liverpool, we went straight to Dublin where my mother now lived and where we still had some relatives. Now I have never been much of a politician and Irish politics has always baffled me, however, one of the first things I noticed on getting home was a poster which read 'Irish ship sunk in English Convoy'. I was still puzzling this out when I met a very friendly taxi driver who said he would be delighted to take us to Blackrock. When my wife saw the dilapidated taxi she said sadly, *"Why ever did you take this old wreck? I was really looking forward to my first taxi."* I said, *"I felt sorry for the poor fellow."* She was not amused.

There were lots of funny stories to balance the tragedies, as Dublin too had its bomb. There were airmen interned at the Curragh, and one of the stories doing the rounds was that on landing in the middle of the camp, the guard ran up to the astonished pilot and said, *"You are in luck Sir, for the gun is up in Dublin being mended."*

Most of the young farmers had joined the Local Defense Force. They were ready to protect the country from any invader, or this was their intention. However, they had not seen Hitler's plan for the invasion of Ireland, and I suspect Ireland would have collapsed in a few hours. I saw some of these maps later when I was in Germany and was amazed at the detail and precision of their scheme. Ireland had no navy or air force to speak of and they were very innocent, these young farmers, and luckily, they did not have to put it to the test.

We listened to all the armchair critics and helped to pick the apples at my mother-in-law's garden in the country, and then one day I received a letter from the War Office asking me to come and see them. Even though we had been expecting this each day, when it did come my wife almost fell out of the apple tree. Anyway, we duly bid farewell to Ireland and arrived in London in the autumn. The blackout was in full force, and we made our way to where my sister-in-law (with her two small boys) lived in a cottage in the woods near Guildford. When we arrived in this dark corner of the wood, we saw a small light waving about. This was Margery with a small half-shaded torch with its regulation blackout. I shall never forget how kind she was, all alone with her two small boys and a couple of dachshunds.

A few weeks later they packed up to leave the cottage and I was helping to get some hens into a crate. Unfortunately, as I was doing so, the dogs decided to help me out with the hens and killed one of the birds in the process! I said to my sister and her son, *"Not to worry, I'll bury it."* But the ground was hard with frost, and I had some difficulty digging a hole. As I was making slow progress, all of a sudden, I realised that I was not in the tropics, that meat was rationed and chicken very scarce. So, we ended up eating the hen! That incident reminds me of a similar one in Iraq, where someone mistakenly shot a grey crane, believing it to be a bustard. It too was buried and later when someone arrived and said it was very good eating, we dug up the grey crane and had it cooked.

We bought bicycles, which neither of us had ridden for many years, but we soon found out the great pleasure of pedaling about and having time to look and see all sorts of things that one never sees in a car. There's nothing better than learning the geography of London on a bike.

My brother Brian came to see us and brought the girl he was going to marry. Brian had been born when I was in France in 1918. By now he was a Captain in Princess Louise's Own Regiment. So far in the war, he'd been engaged on coastal defense with a machinegun battery, as the Battle of Britain had raged in the skies above him; and with everyone expecting a full-scale invasion at any minute. He had seen some very strange things and had loads of stories to share. Thankfully, he looked well, and I was very taken with my future sister-in-law.

Chapter 15

Joining Royal Engineers as 2ⁿᵈ Lieutenant

I re-joined the army on December 31ˢᵗ, 1941, as a 2ⁿᵈ Lieutenant in the Royal Engineers. After donning my new uniform and heading out of barracks, a street urchin called out, *"Hey, Grandpa on a bike!"* Despite this taunt, I was proud of my new uniform and proud to be back in the services. By this stage in the war, big changes had occurred in the lives of most of my siblings and relatives. As I said, my brother Brian had seen action with a machine gun battery during the battle of Britain. My other brother Douglas, who had gone to Ceylon before the war as a missionary and became Rector of Christ Church Galle Face in Colombo, was now a Chaplain to the Navy and his young family were growing up in Ceylon.

My brother-in-law Donald was by then a Captain in the Irish Guards and would have been a success in whatever he did. His lovely sense of humour had lost nothing of its magic when he told us of his first day's training with this noble regiment – how he had offered to pay for a hair-cut 'which would not frighten his wife', only to find that his head had been shaved! When one of his friends looked at him, he quipped, *"I am glad I didn't pay for mine."*

Donald was instructing at some top-secret Allied school of gunnery and had friends among the Polish and Czechs and others who were attached to the school. He found that although many of his friends did not really like each other very much, what they did have in common was a deep loathing for Hitler and the Nazis.

Burton, my next brother-in-law, who had gone to South Africa, because he was too delicate to spend another winter in England, was by then an Observer with the S.A.A.F., and was a C.3 on Coastal Patrol.

As for myself, well it was really quite funny to be drilling again. I had to present arms, and deliver a message with a cane, and this did seem to me quite comical after so many years of civilian life. However, I was not the only 'old boy' doing it.

I was sent to Chester where we lived in an impoverished sort of barracks, and the bunk beds seemed to have mattresses stuffed with hay. Each time the fellow on the top level turned over, the man below got a shower of hay on his face. The whole place was wired so that when the doors were opened, the lights went out. Blackout regulation! For the first few days we were all rather amused when each time one of the forty or so officers opened the door to go to the bathroom, not only did the lights go out, but the electric razor (which many people used sitting on their bed) would also stop working. I frequently spent the night with my wife who was at the Blossoms Hotel.

Photo of Daphne and I (back in uniform) in 1942

I was posted to R.E. Transportation, this meant 'Engineer officers with knowledge of railway work'. I made a trip to Snowdon to inspect the narrow-gauge railway which was going to be used in conjunction with the Commando School. Although I would have liked to have been seconded to this school, the war office would not agree. After that, I was sent to a place near Shrewsbury, where Major George was in charge, and they were repairing the Shropshire and Montgomery Railway. On the bridge over the Severn, I found that some of the cross girders were lying there not bolted to anything.

Our Colonel was an Irishman and I liked him very much. One day when we were talking about Ireland, he said to me,

"Of course you and I are different religions". To this, I replied, *"No, I don't think so, my father was a parson,"*

"Oh yes, I know that, but I am a Presbyterian."

I had never thought on those lines, but he came from the North of Ireland.

When 1ˢᵗ April 1942 came around, I could not resist it; and arriving at the camp in the early morning I awakened them all saying, *"You had better hurry up as the Colonel is on the square waiting."* There was a wild dash to get dressed and out to the parade ground, which was some distance away. I went along too, and, on the way, I saw a sapper who seemed to have nothing to do, so I said to him, *"Here, hold onto this dustbin lid as there is a wild cat in the bin."* I really was amazed when he did just that. By now I was getting rather apprehensive as I had not expected my joke to work as well. I must say they were all awfully nice about it and we had a good laugh.

The Colonel came in one day and said to me, "Would you like a job at the War office?" I am afraid my reply was not very tactful: *"Well, if I could modernise some of the training in bridging* [which I considered old fashioned], *I would like the job very much."* This was definitely the wrong thing to say, and I was duly posted to India.

I went out on a troopship in convoy, with the whole jaunt taking ten weeks, which included several weeks at Durban, where the people were most awfully kind. After all the security we had been taught in England, I was astonished at the careless chat I overheard there about ships coming and going – the taxi drivers knew everything or so it seemed to me.

When I arrived at Delhi as a Lieutenant, I was interviewed by two Brigadiers who were Royal Engineers. They were concerned with the re-building of bridges in Burma and Malaysia, which was just the sort of thing I was interested in. I was shown the lists of bridging equipment required for the re-building of these bridges and I noticed they had ordered pile-driver frames from England and pile hammers from America. I knew that this was a mistake. I said, *"The pile-driver frames in England have only 6 inches between leads, and the American hammer requires 27 inches, they will be quite useless."* Later when I was a Lieutenant Colonel, I found hundreds of these American hammers at a place called Panneghar – all quite useless – so obviously my advice had not been taken.

Either way, I was sent on to Jallundah and there I met Colonel Gordon, who asked me to have some talks with the officers who had come along and would be going into Burma. My job was to try and find out how much they really did know about bridging. As far as I was concerned, these talks produced some very surprising results. One or two people had claimed to have built not only some of my bridges in Iraq, but also some of the bridges that I had worked on in Brazil. It was a fortunate thing that I was there to sort them out.

Colonel Gordon then asked me to start a bridging school, with the first priority being to find a suitable place, that it should be within 100 miles of Calcutta and that it must be on the railway. Highly delighted with this assignment, I then went off in the direction of Jamahadpur, and having had a good look around, I eventually found a place which had all the things I was looking for: moderately high ground, a fair drop into the river and an open space where we could launch girders on to open country.

I started immediately to collect materials that I would need for this project, and I also met Colonel Clutterbuck, who was satisfied with the site. However, he did point out that it had been condemned by the Health Authorities. The next time I went there I found that it was full of mosquitoes. To try and fix this problem, as soon as the construction company arrived, we put high octane spirit in the pools over a wide area and killed all the flies and mosquitoes. At least there would be no danger of malaria at the school in the immediate future.

We were very lucky in having a man called Fitzgerald as the Director and another man named Hill as Chief Engineer of the nearby H.Q. of the Bengal and Nagpur Railway. Both of them were extremely helpful and both hailed from Dublin. Without their help the school would have been in a bad way, as they allowed me to choose anything that I needed for the school from their store. I was in my element, and chose pile drivers, pile driver hammers, boilers, timber and a great quantity of other useful material.

Unfortunately, my enthusiasm did not extend to the construction company which had come to help me start the school. In a serious manner, I told them at length of the importance of it, but they were not very receptive and left everything to the Indian officers. With this slackness, I said I would have to report them to Delhi. Since I was by then only a Captain, they thought my threat rather amusing, as their C.O. was a Major. When I did report them for slackness, a Colonel Yates was sent down to shake them up, and none of them spoke amicably to me for some time afterwards.

The school was now under way and bridging was arriving, as well as companies for training. There were Callender Hamilton spans and Bailey bridging that we would use for instruction in the school, and later to go into Burma as it became possible. My majority came through and I was sent back to Jallundah as the commanding officer of a company of Indian Engineers, who wore topies instead of uniform hats. In fact, they looked more like racing drivers than soldiers. When I asked them why they were wearing these topies, they said they thought they might get more pay if they wore topies. I said, *"Look here, you are Indian soldiers and I think you should wear your puggaree."* But they did not like my suggestion and some of them continued to wear the topie. I thought the rifle drill might put an end to this, and that is what we had. Down flat on your face, up again, down again, up down, up down. After this they all agreed to wear their puggarees.

They were great fellows, the best bridging men one could get; Indians from Bombay who'd been involved in bridging and boats all their lives. I had known many of their fathers in Iraq, and one was the son of Bahna, a splendid man we had at Barbuti in 1933. Yes, there were many names in that company I already knew well.

When this company got to the bridging school at Rakha Mines and we told them about knots, we found that they knew more about knots than had ever been written in a military handbook – tying up timber, erecting sheer legs, gin poles, cross beams, derricks and cranes – they knew it all and would go up a 12 inch by 12 inch timber 30 or 40 feet with no difficulty. It gave me enormous pleasure to be with such very skilled men again.

116

By the way, in case anyone thinks it is a drink, a gin pole is a single pole with ties on the top and is erected to lift awkward equipment. The pole is held to the ground with an anchor. Sheer legs are 12 inch by 12 inch timbers about 40 feet long, on which one slings a hammer to drive piles and move various things.

By the time we were ready to go to the school at Rakha Mines, we knew each other pretty well, and when I was alone, they would say, *"Salaam Gee,"* instead of saluting smartly. When the big day arrived and I was to march them up to the school, since the C. O. was very fond of parades, he had three companies lined up to receive us. We had some good pipers in the company and we marched in playing 'The wearing of the Green'. It was not a good idea, since I am afraid *"That most distressful country of Ireland"* (to quote the C.O.) had no happy memories for him.

From the school at Rakha, one could often witness lightning on the hills opposite, as it always struck at the same spot, because of the copper in the ground. It reminded me of the Rider Haggard's 'Witches dance of death'.

At that time the line between Lumding and Manipur Road was only single track, so by now the traffic had become very heavy and the line would have to be doubled. As a result, I was sent up to look at some of the bridges. There were numerous rivers with many bridges of about 100 and 150-foot spans, and the construction job required 90 pile drivings.

Although Delhi had promised to send everything we needed, nothing arrived, so we had to improvise in all directions. For example, we got a company to make a pile driving frame out of an old railway bogie. One of the railway workshops made us a drop-hammer, which was in ten sections and could be used according to the weight required. With suitable bolts it would even make a two-ton hammer, which was quite clever and made for easy handling.

L.F. Jackson, the Chief Engineer of the Bengal and Assam Railway lived at Saipur. I called on him, and needless to say, we talked about bridging. He was very interested in the work I had done in Iraq and Brazil. Mr. Jackson showed me the plans he had for a bridge over the Brahmaputra, which cost about £4 million, and would have 10,400-foot spans. I looked at the plan for some time, which comprised twin-cylinder piers and would go a great depth into the river. From this, I had the impression that the foundations would be overloaded. I told Mr. Jackson what I thought and was quite astonished when he said simply, *"Will you take on building this bridge?"*

"Of course, I would love to, but…" I added reluctantly, *"I am in the army and I will have to see what they want me to do in Assam."* After that things moved quickly and Jackson spoke to Delhi, telling them what he wanted and arguing that this was more urgent than anything they might have for me to do. There and then I was appointed Chief Engineer for the Brahmaputra Bridge.

The bridge had been designed by London Consultants – though I never knew who they were – and had been agreed by the India Railway Board. The steel work was by Braithwaite, Burns and Jessop and the foundations were by the Hindustan Construction Company. So far, I had only seen the plans, and upon my appointment, I immediately went up to the proposed site of the bridge. The river here was tremendous, seven times the size of the Rhine; and in flood time the Rhine's flow was just a fraction of that of the Ganges, which had a flow rate of several million cubic feet per second and with scour records of 100 feet.

Near the site of the bridge there was a ferry which took railway trucks between Amigon and Gauhati for many years, and it seemed to work quite well. I also found out that the work on the approach embankments, and the minor bridging in them, was almost complete. I did not approve of the way the trial borings had been taken, as these had been wash-borings. Though they had been taken right across the bed of the river, they only showed sand and gravel, even at 100 feet. I thought that if the scour records in the Ganges were 100 feet, in this river we must have a penetration of at least 150 feet. My figures showed a loading of 11 tons per square foot on their plan.

Incorporated in the design of the twin cylinders piers, there was a scheme for converting from open caisson to pneumatic sinking, in case it should become necessary. This would have necessitated putting a plate across – inside the walls – to allow for compressed air. I thought that it would have been impossible to fix this plate inside the wells, as there would be so little room. To do this a diver would have to get in wearing diving boots, and I knew for certain that I could not do it.

Having seen the river I was more convinced than ever that this design with its twin cylinder piers was most unsuitable, since the scour stirred up by the up-stream cylinder would cause heavy erosion against the second cylinder. I duly told Mr. Jackson that I was very worried about several aspects of the design. Jackson called a meeting of everyone involved with the bridge to hear what I had to say. While most of them disagreed with me, one person (the Chief Engineer of Braithwaite, Burns and Jesson) was in full agreement, namely, that the bridge in its present form had to be stopped.

At the meeting, I was asked how I thought it should be designed, so, I made a rough sketch and suggested that the piers would have hollow walls; and that the caissons would be splayed out, and in these caissons, there would be 2-inch piping to be used for jetting to speed up the sinking. My design allowed for 150 feet of penetration below the bed of the river, and this would have meant 6 tons a square foot, compared with 11 tons a square foot, as the original diagram showed. If the original plan had gone ahead, it would require 22,000 tons of concrete in each pier. Given the fact that the caissons would take seven months to construct, and that the army wanted the bridge finished in a year, the project was not possible. I think this was one of the most painful decisions I ever had to make, and many people were hurt by it. However, it would have been a major calamity if the bridge had collapsed – so I stuck by my guns!

Usually when I went to Calcutta, I stayed at the Bengal Club and always called on my friends Ian and Nady Tainah, who were most awfully kind and listened to all my worries. On this occasion I think they realized how important the bridge assignment was for me. Apart from the honour of being offered this huge bridge to build, with all the responsibility involved, I had also planned to get my wife to fly out, as I would be in one place until the job was finished, and several people did have their wives with them.

It was something of a relief when I was posted off to look at another bridge that was causing some anxiety. At least I could stop thinking about the vexed questions surrounding the building of the Brahmaputra bridge. You see during this period they were also building a bridge over the Beki River and the engineer in charge had some difficult caissons to sink. This was a very fast-flowing river, and they wanted me to go down and see if this work could be speeded up. Anyway, I telephoned through to the Bengal and Assan Railway, spoke to a very nice fellow called Martin and asked him whether the engineer doing the bridge was any good at his job. Martin said, *"We like him a lot. He's a great favourite and our best cricketer."* Not being a cricketer myself, I thought this was a joke, but Martin was quite serious about it.

At any rate, I went on to see the bridge and upon seeing the Beki River for the first time was surprised by how vicious it was. I met the cricketing-engineer, and he gave me a warm welcome. I was a Major at the time, and he called me 'old man'. After analysing the project, I felt he had underestimated this assignment. I asked him what hours were being worked, and he said he thought they would do it easily, they were working nine hours a day. I then asked if I could see his sinking diagram, which is the chart that most engineers would have before they start. It shows the different times taken in each step of the building process, from the caisson sinking to the times taken in sand or clay, the concreting, the sinking, the movement of plant and the erection of forms, and so on. Well, when our cricketer answered me that he'd never heard of it, I got very worried, and felt I must find out more about the river in flood. There was an aerodrome fairly near, so I asked if they could help me to find out about the floods?

Eventually a large and friendly Squadron Leader took me up in a little 'Oster' plane. We were both so big that I really wondered if this little plane could get off the ground, but we did and we flew towards the Himalayas. From this we could see that two rivers had joined up and formed the Beki and that it was a big river indeed. The total span of the new bridge was only about 1000 feet. It was a very important one, replacing the old bridge which had become unsafe and could not take the amount of water coming through.

When I got back and wrote my report, I said in no uncertain terms that I felt that this bridge would never be finished in time and might affect the supply lines to the 12th and 14th armies. Since I could not make Delhi understand my concern, I decided to go direct to the head of the American detachment, a General Yaunt, who was in charge of all transportation. He was a first class 'Westpoint' man and a fine engineer. After he listened to what I had to say, he then called up my two Brigadiers and we went over the details. General Yaunt realised the urgency and agreed that we must get on with three eight-hour shifts immediately. This was done and the bridge was only just ready before the flood came, and the old bridge had to be closed. There are times when one has to risk great unpopularity if one is quite sure that the project is important, and this was one such situation. For whatever reason, I seem to have an affinity for getting myself into such situations.

By the way, the cancellation of the Brahmaputra bridge remained in my mind for years; the enormity of that river, the annual flooding and devastation, as well as the frequent droughts, all made me long to do something to control even a small part of these waters.

Years later I returned to West Pakistan once again in 1952, when I had to inspect a dam on the Indus. Each time I visited that part of Asia, I had some impression of the enormity of the Himalayas. As the Brahmaputra rises in Tibet at the back of these mountains, I think it should be possible to construct tunnels to take off some of the surplus water. It could possibly be used on the plains of India for hydro-electric power and for irrigation. My idea was that these tunnels would be placed at strategic intervals of about 100 miles. Although the cost would be enormous, nevertheless it would be offset by the calamitous damage caused by annual flooding. I talked of this topic with all my friends and any people I felt might have some influence, but unfortunately my ideas remained just that, never becoming reality. Perhaps if I'd met Mrs. Gandhi or Chou en-Lai in my later life, I might have been able to convince them of the merits of the idea, but that's all conjecture!

In January 1945, I took about 10 days leave and went down to see my brother Douglas and his family in Colombo, Ceylon. I was overwhelmed by just how beautiful the place was, and in a way, I felt they were lucky to be there. While in Colombo, I spent a lot of the time in the water with my relations, engaged in really lovely bathing in a clear cool sea. I can remember losing my ring and then being able to see it on the bottom quite clearly. Unfortunately, it was not so easy for me to swim down and pick it up.

My memory of the Church was a very cheerful place with a good choir seating about 400 people and being quite full. Most of the congregation were Naval people (with many senior officers in attendance), and I remember a Wren I met telling me that Douglas never preached a dull sermon. My sister-in-law ran the Royal Navy school in Colombo, as a lot of people had their families out there. The city also had five cinemas and a zoo, and the cooler hills were always a good place to visit during the very hot weather. From Colombo, I was able to get a flight back to Calcutta, which was much better than the long hot journey by train. Reaching the city, I had a streaming cold and do not remember much about it.

As regards my brother Douglas, having spent much of my life abroad, I had missed getting to know him when he was young (since he was nine years younger than me). He graduated from Trinity College Dublin, where many of our forebears had been and which I've always regretted not having attended. For a time, he taught at a school in Dublin and then he decided to go into the Church. So, he went back to Trinity in 1931 and got a First Class Honours, as well as the Archbishop King's Prize in 1933. I didn't know this until after his death when he was 61. He was a most loveable person, and we were all very proud of him.

Getting back to my war years in India, I remember that at one stage amoebic dysentery was devastating our Company, with us losing about 30%. When about six Indian cooks went down with it, I immediately suspected carelessness. I duly conducted an extra inspection and as a warning, I gave a Field

Punishment No. 1 to the men. When after a few minutes they all pretended to be dead, I ordered that water be thrown over them. When they then lay there without moving, I said, *"Bury them!"* After the first bucket of sand was thrown over them, they were all on their feet and consequently, I believe we had cleaner cookhouses thereafter.

One of our officers, a major in the Indian Engineers, had a small house and as there was a tree growing rather too near, he came along to ask if my fellows who had been clearing things away with a hand winch, could come along and deal with the tree. I sent along the sappers and put it out of my mind for the time being. Sometime later he called to say that he now had no house, as the sappers had pulled the tree down on top of it. I couldn't help laughing and he soon started laughing as well.

Chapter 16

Lumding, the Jap threat, Burma bridge inspection and V. E. Day

Lumding, which was about 50 miles west of Kohima and about 70 miles to the north of Imphal, was the railway junction for Chittagong and all the supplies for the 12th and 14th armies came by train through it. This meant that about 90% of the supplies going over the 'Hump' were passing through Lumding, and no doubt the Japs knew this. Between March and July 1944, the battle of Imphal raged, as Imphal was besieged by the Japs. Now what has always amazed me was why the Japs didn't attack Lumding at the same time? As far as the Maninore Road, it was mostly virgin jungle, so if they had got in there it would have been very hard to get them out.

I remember a young staff Captain coming along to see us and telling us, *"You must all fight to the last man."* He also said that there were 1000 well-armed Japs coming along, and that he thought they would be here in a day, or at the most two days. We had a battery to the north of us, and I began to think that they were rather too quiet. So, I walked along to the ridge (from where we could see them) to check if everything was alright. To my amazement, I discovered that they had all gone.

When I asked our staff captain why they had been moved, he replied, *"Oh well, we did not want them caught in the bag."*

"But your instructions are – you must all fight to the last man!"

I was very angry about this, and said, *"Look here, we are a bridging company of Indian Engineers. We have about five Bren guns and not more than twenty-five rifles. I think it would be much better if we get in behind them and cut their communications."*

He did not agree with this and said that our job was to defend the place *"to the last man."* He then left, which was just as well.

At that moment I realised that those of us who had been at Passchendaele in the 1914-18 war would always be in some way different from this younger generation. Unlike myself, they had not witnessed first-hand the useless destruction of the first war, where thousands were slaughtered in battles like Passchendaele. Despite the slaughter, places like Passchendaele did breed a fellowship which has never been surpassed.

When I was at Jallundah I met a Major called Battersby, who had built a lot of the bridges up to the Darjeeling hill station. Naturally, we talked a lot about bridging, and I think it must have been in that connection that later on – when I was Commandant of the bridging school at Rakha Mines – I received a telegram telling me to go down to Burma as soon as possible, to advise about the rebuilding of their railway bridges.

Of course, I went straight away. On the way to Rangoon,

I met a Brigadier also going down there who had a lot of plans for bridging work. After examining his plans, I did not think they were suitable; they would have been better in London. For example, they talked about using a camel's foot, which is a big casting with a screw elevator, to raise or lower the girder. Now this method was fine for using in a solid foundation like a road, but in Burma it was utterly useless, as we would require piles with probably a 40-foot penetration. So, his plans had to be scrapped, as these deep Burmese rivers were a very different proposition from European ones.

When I arrived in Rangoon, I met Brigadier Herbert (Resident Engineer and also head of transportation), my old friend Battersby; and also Major Hawtrey (a district engineer from the Burma railway), who was a very experienced engineer and later became Chief Engineer of the Crown Agents. I was asked to inspect the Rangoon-Prohme line first and later the Rangoon-Mandalay line. On one of the damaged bridges on the Rangoon-Prohme line, a through-span was not properly supported and could cause derailment. For this reason, I had to close the line. Fortunately, this closure did not last long.

I was very fortunate to have Major Hawtrey with me, as he knew all about bridging. We would start out on a special sort of jeep with steel wheels for the railway track, or they could be removed, and ordinary tyres put on. This was very useful, because when we found that the Jap had removed the track, we could change from steel to ordinary wheels and then travel by road, making a detour back to the railway. Usually, the Jap held onto one place and did not move about very much on the railway.

I think I went to Burma three times, and during these visits I saw about 20 major bridges (between 100 and 500-feet spans) that had been very badly damaged by bombing. In some cases, it was nearly impossible to see what the bridge had been, and at one particular place the spans had been blown upside down and right away from the bridge. We could not help thinking that one or two spans would have been enough, and not smash up the whole bridge. Either way, the Americans and ourselves had made a good demolishing job of it. Hawtrey knew what had been there beforehand and was often amazed at what we found.

I distinctly remember how at the Pyu river bridge, one third of the span had been blown about 50 feet away from the abutment. Now it took one hell of a bomb force to do that! I also recall how the Waw bridge showed just the remains of a box girder. Without Hawtrey telling me what it was like beforehand, it was virtually impossible to visualise what it had once been.

One of the greatest problems repairing bombed bridges was having to deal with the wreckage of the original bridge. At the school we taught our officers how to make earth anchors and put in 10 hand winches. In this way they could pull out the original steel work and save time. Also, it was pretty obvious that pile driving was a very reasonable method for bridging, and that these engineering companies had to be taught as much as possible about it, as far as it can be taught in a school.

We also considered that cantilever erection was very often the most effective method. For example, we sometimes used the Callender Hamilton Span bridge, which is a modular portable prefabricated truss bridge (invented by a Kiwi named Hamilton during the 1930's). Similarly, we often used the Bailey Girder Bridge, which is also a portable prefabricated truss bridge, which was developed early in the war by the British. The great thing about the Bailey girder was it required no special tools or heavy equipment to assemble. Whereas the Callender Hamilton was designed for heavier loading and was therefore more suitable for railways. In fact, it was so good that the bridges put there (during the war) are still in good shape to this day (as I dictate my story). We were able to cantilever up to 200 feet spans over various rivers with the C.H. girders. In addition, the photographs I took of the different bridges we erected were a great help to officers in training, and gave them some idea of what they would be dealing with when they did get into Burma proper.

I remember once I met a Company of very enthusiastic African engineers, who were all great fellows, and I was full of admiration for them. Once, they were doing their best to pull some mangled steelwork out of the river, but they really should have used some 10-ton winches to do the job. I had put down one of these bridges for replacement, but this Colonel (an extremely nice fellow) said cheerfully, *"I can get that girder straightened up and riveted by the men."* I then asked him if his African men knew how to rivet.

"I can train them in no time," he replied.

Hearing that, I eventually persuaded him that it would be better to scrap these girders. Although those Africans were full of enthusiasm, it was asking too much.

During this period, although Hawtrey and I were trying to inspect as many bridges as possible, nevertheless the military police kept holding us up, arguing that the Jap was far too near for comfort. One day I, thinking I was being clever, got away without the police seeing us. We had a lovely run through open country and did not see anyone. When we arrived back to HQ at the town near the Letpadan bridge, they were astonished to see us, as we were completely surrounded by the enemy. Why the Jap let us through, I never knew! On that particular occasion, the Japs attacked us at nighttime, but thankfully nothing much happened. As we were delayed for a couple of days, we had plenty of time to examine the Letpaden bridge and decide what to do with it.

At around the same time, Delhi had asked for a report on the Salween River bridge, and just before I had gone up, I went along to see my old friend Bob Mansergh, who was by now the Major General of a fifth Indian division. I had last seen him in Iraq when he was a Captain and came out hunting boar. Seeing me after all the long year, General Mansergh said, *"You must get these bridges of yours going as soon as possible, because we have to take away our wounded in jeeps over these awful roads – we urgently need the railway."* I replied, *"Well, there is only one more bridge that I must see and that is this bridge over the Salween."* This made him laugh a lot and he said, *"What does Delhi think? We have been trying to get on to the Salween bridge for the last month and the Japs are still holding it. How do you imagine you are going to get there?"* Of course, we did not. On our failed attempt to reach Salween, I shall always remember the old saloon we chose to sleep in, it was full of bullet holes, and as it was pouring rain we got drenched. We could hear firing in the distance and that was as near as we got to the Salween.

I was very impressed by this beautiful country and its beautiful women, and it always puzzled me to see them sitting in a circle brushing each other's hair. Another thing I remember was the priests passing by with a huge bodyguard, perhaps twenty men all carrying a very sharp knife called a Dha. I was not taking risks with the bodyguard and would keep them covered with my revolver under my coat, in case they misused the Dha on my head!

Back at Rakha Mines we were having a bad time with mosquitoes and, in spite of all the spraying, they came back. We had the bashas sprayed with D.D.T., but we could see them coming in by twenties and thirties at sunrise and sunset, with the little silent ones being the worst. We took our Mepacrine and didn't worry too much, as it was just one of many problems we faced.

Although peace came to Europe in May 1945, as we were still in Burma fighting the Jap, we felt that our war was not over yet, and as yet we did not know about the atom bomb. As everyone knows, the first such bomb was dropped on Hiroshima city on August 6th, 1945, and the second three days later on Nagasaki city on August 9th. V. J. Day or Victory Japan Day was on September 2nd, 1945, when the Japs surrendered, and consequently my war was finally over. As a result, I left Rakha Mines on September 11th, 1945, for Declali, having handed over to my relief. I went up to Ranchi over the ghat road, which winds the whole way over a 3000-foot range and is all extremely beautiful. I was hoping to find an old friend Tutton, but he had gone sometime before. Ranchi was cool and dry, and I went to the cinema there.

After Ranchi, I went on to Calcutta. Since the war was officially over, there were all sorts of rumours about demobbing, but none of us really knew when we would get out of the services. In Calcutta they were showing 'Burma Objective', with the emphasis on how the U.S. had won the war in Burma. It spoke well for the British Tommy in the cinema that he did not throw a brick at it!

Chapter 17

Return to London, leave in Ireland, and joining Central Commission in Germany and the Essen Railway team for four years (1945-49)

The three months between V.E. Day and V.J. Day were a bit of an anti-climax, with the war ending very quickly in the end. I flew home with my suitcase full of little presents made in India, and at one of the stops – I think Palestine – I bought a bottle of whisky, which leaked over everything and smelt like a bar. However, nothing mattered, I was alive, at home and my wife and I were together again. Although I was still bright yellow from the Mepacrine, people nevertheless said I looked very well.

My old friend M.G. Lubbock had retired from Brazil, and then done something he'd always wanted to do – settling in a prime hunting county in Ireland. He had bought a nice old place near Fermoy, County Cork, and almost the best part of the old place was the stabling. Here he had several good horses, which he rode as often as there was a 'Meet of Hounds' that he could get to.

I went to Ireland on leave and spent a few days with M.G.L., and he showed me his house with pride and his horses with affection. We talked into the night and caught up on all the time that had passed since we had left him in Brazil. We also drove out to see the hunt and enjoy the Irish scene, which he seemed to fit into so well. He had made a lot of friends, and he looked well and happy. When we got back to his large rambling house, we sat around an enormous fire where every bit of heat went up the chimney each time he went in and out of the room. For whatever reason he seemed to have toughened up more than I had and didn't notice the cold.

The grounds of this old place were a natural fox covert and sometimes the hounds would meet there. It was a splendid covert, as the old rhododendrons had been there for perhaps a hundred years, and he told us that on one occasion the fox – followed by the whole pack of hounds – had gone through the house. He was delighted, and I think only sorry that the riders and horses had not been able to follow.

There seemed to be a great many foxes, and I heard plenty of terrible tales of their destruction of the hens. As a result, there wasn't an egg in sight to eat! From what I heard, I don't think there was much hunting during the war years, even in Ireland.

At that time, it seemed as if the occupation of Germany would continue for a long time. The central Commission was being formed, so I applied and was duly interviewed by a couple of Brigadiers. Since Railway engineering was my choice, I was sent to Essen on the Control Team. I think I can safely say that no railway had had such a hammering as that particular area. The infamous or famous (depending on your viewpoint) Krupps Works was in the middle and there were Allied air-raid targets all around. In a nutshell, most of the area was bombed to smithereens!

The Control Team was appointed to get the railway working as quickly and as economically as possible. Although the railway team was British, at Essen we had French, Belgian and Americans on the Commission. Each team had a controller, and the sections were audit, traffic, police and engineering. I was in charge of engineering. From the start we were in opposition to the Germans, because they did not want us economizing with our money.

We had a staff of bi-lingual Germans, who for one reason or another were anxious to work with us. The two inspectors who accompanied me were very understanding and knowledgeable and we got on splendidly. One of them had been in Sweden during most of the war and they were both railway men with engineering degrees. The office staff were men and women, and the secretaries and typists were very efficient and with a good understanding of English.

In 1945-1946 they were still hungry in Germany, and more so in Essen, where the devastation was so appalling. We could get tea, coffee and cigarettes, which all had enormous value on the black market, but our army rations were derisory. I distinctly remember a large army vehicle delivering the following rations for 2 people (my wife and I) for 3 days: half a pound of smoked haddock, half a cabbage, 3 ounces of butter and 4 ounces of cheese. This meagre fare was, if I remember correctly, not unusual. Also, we were not allowed to buy at the German shops. In fact, there was almost nothing to buy for money. In a nutshell, Germany was very hungry at the time.

The house I was allotted had belonged to a German Naval Captain, Captain Rose, who had moved to a small cottage he'd built nearby. Naturally he did not want to move, but we paid him a reasonable rent and were on friendly terms. He had lost one son – killed in Russia – and another son was in one-man submarines during the war. Also, his youngest son was just leaving Salem, the famous Scottish school which later became Gordonstoun. He was part of the old German establishment, which was still in being. Captain Rose took some of his furniture and we were allotted army furnishings and blankets. My wife arrived over from England with the earlier wives, with their transportation being arranged on a basis of length of separation (ours being four years).

We began with one maid who had been in a concentration camp, and later we employed another younger girl to help. I remember how once the maids had a battle over a single cup of rice, and it was from such incidents that I learnt just how much food meant to these women (who thought nothing of injuring each other to get it). Such incidents also showed just how much the war had brutalized ordinary people. Later we had a laundress visit our abode twice a week. Her husband had been killed when a bomb destroyed their small green-grocers shop. She now lived in a tiny hut where they used to store potatoes.

400 wives, belonging to all ranks, travelled by ship from Harwich to Cuxhaven. Many had never left England before and were very apprehensive. Most had heard of 'lovely German wines' and expected to have them served. Instead,

what they got was Naffi tea in a thick white cup, having queued up for ages for it.

On the ships, wives with more than two children were given the cabins, and wives with no children shared a deck, slept in double decker bunks, their 'ablutions' performed on another deck, and with no luxury whatsoever – all very egalitarian. As for my own wife, it took three days for her to get to the Ruhr. I happily recall how she cheerfully arrived with a huge bundle of lamp shade frames, since I had told her about the draped and fringed affair which hung over our dining table.

The Ruhr, in spite of all the coal mining and steel furnaces, was actually very beautiful: beech woods had been planted to screen the ugliness, and there were countless artificial lakes for boating and bathing. Krupp had made a splendid lake near his house – the 'Villa Hugel' – which was nearly three miles long and one third of a mile wide. The lake had been formed by a weir in the river. There was a small yacht clubhouse and some very nice boats, which we took full advantage of. This being one of the few 'perks' for having won the war.

At that time in the Ruhr, there were about 400 bridges destroyed and one of my worries was finding materials to rebuild or repair them. I would ask, *"Have you any steel anywhere in Germany?"* We needed girders, angles and flange plates, but the answer was always that there was nothing, that it had all been used or destroyed. Anyway, one day I noticed that a girder had been off-loaded at a place called Martin. I distinctly remember the name, as I have a nephew called Martin. When I determined to see the place, suddenly every possible obstacle was put in my way, no road, no train, etc. However, as the obstacles increased, so did my curiosity to get to the root of what was going on. Finally, I got there with my two inspectors, and we found 2500 tons of steel hidden away, all the angles and flange plates that we needed so badly. This was all very baffling, and at the time I couldn't help thinking, *"Why are they concealing these stores? Is it for the black market? Or is it to get more out of the Allies?"*

Another similar example was when a huge requisition was lodged for electrical equipment. I said, *"Surely we have masses of such equipment here in our store. It couldn't have been all destroyed or used up in the war."* When I was told it had all been used up, I immediately asked to inspect the store. Once again, all sorts of difficulties and obstacles were placed in my way – but I kept at it, and we eventually found the place full of valuable equipment.

What was the reason for all this deception? I think that a great many Germans wanted to make England and America pay through the nose to rebuild their country, regardless of the delay involved, or the utter misery that their people were enduring in that frightful winter of 1945-46. Many railway stations were without roofs and thousands of windows were without glass. Although allegedly there wasno glass in Germany, nevertheless at one place I found miles of glass hidden away. It had been covered with those brushes normally used to sweep up the snow. Feeling very foolish, I said, *"Take away those brushes,"* and there was all the glass I needed. I also remember that in another instance, when I insisted on looking into an enormous filing cabinet, I found the files were full of nails. I hope that someone else felt foolish, or did they? I never knew. Perhaps this sort of thing is natural enough after a war, but as none of us had these materials and all Europe needed them at the time, it was infuriating to be constantly deceived.

On the plus side of post-war Germany, the country was full of game, and I engaged in the most wonderful pheasant shooting. The Gordon Highlanders were stationed at Essen, and J.B. Gerrard (who was Colonel of the 1ˢᵗ Battalion) was a very good shot. We went shooting together and often brought back five or six brace of pheasants, which we gave to our friends and our German neighbours; even once gifting a pheasant to our naval Captain and his son. On that specific occasion, upon reaching Captain Rose's abode, I looked around for a doorbell and was surprised to see a ship's bell hanging near the door marked S.S. Grimsby. I did not ring it, since instead they saw me and came out, cheerfully saying, *"Good morning."* They then told me that there was some splendid news in the paper – Germany would fight another war, with England on its side, against Russia and this time they would win. As you might have guessed, words failed me! I left the pheasant and went home.

Captain Rose was really a very unusual German. He was one of the few who did not pretend to have hated the Nazis. In fact, to my astonishment, he said, *"I am proud to have served the Fuhrer."* This was his unequivocal reply to a Major in the Gordon Highlanders, whom we had asked to meet him, when the Major said, *"We were so sorry for gentlemen like you having to serve that little Corporal."*

While we lived in Germany one could safely say that each day brought a surprise, and even after four years I felt I did not understand them. At first most of us thought how similar the races are, but as time went by, we felt more and more different.

Most railways have records of locomotive replacements, and these are called bin cards. When I was asked to investigate these records, I found that the railway was being rebuilt and not only in the present time, but for 25 years to come. In addition, I made another discovery in connection with a large quantity of a special ore used in the hardening of steel, which had been taken out of Russia and removed to the Ruhr during the war. Under the reparations agreement it was agreed to return it, however it had not been moved back to Russia and there was a vast file concerning it. When I asked about it I got various replies, such as:

a. That it had all gone.
b. That it had all been used up.
c. That it was not possible to get to the place.
d. That by now it was quite useless.

Once more I insisted on seeing for myself and found that none of these explanations were true. As a result, I made sure that it went to the lawful institution as part of the German reparations.

I am quite sure that in some way we baffled the Germans as much as they baffled us. For example, we had one senior officer who never tired of telling them that we had fought the wrong enemy, as our real enemy was France. In many cases the old-bombed stations, instead of being rebuilt, were being re-modelled and greatly improved. I even remember how in one case one of our senior officers sanctioned the rebuilding of a bridging workshop which had in fact never existed.

As we had friends in England who before the war had friends in Germany, about whom they were anxious, we said we would call on them and take a few simple things like tea, coffee and so on. When we went to visit the German couple, the young wife was charming, and her baby was adorable. The wife had been through a terrifying war, and their beautiful old place was now badly in need of repair. Food was so scarce, that when we arrived, we found her ploughing in the field, hoping to grow potatoes and vegetables.

The couple invited us to 'a simple sort of lunch' – soup and salad from their garden – and the husband apologized that there was no champagne for the party. He explained the Russians had taken it all. In a joking sort of way I said, *"I expect you stole it all from the French."* He replied in all seriousness (not realising I was speaking in jest), *"Naturally we took thousands of bottles meaning to celebrate victory."* I felt very embarrassed for him.

There were a great many hares in Germany, and they made a very good meal. When one day we took one to a neighbour who had a lot of children, she said, *"Thank you, but it is no good to us as we have no butter to cook it."* I think we suggested boiling it.

The word for dinner in German is 'essen', which also means to eat. This was often misunderstood, as they would say, *"We have nothing to eat,"* meaning for dinner. At the time the principal thing lacking was potatoes, since few potatoes had been sown in the war's finale. After the war, many city folk made excursions out to farms, in order to barter, with a pair of shoes or a diamond ring being exchanged for a sack of potatoes.

While in Germany, once we spent a weekend on the island of Nordenay and feasted on beautifully prepared fish, smoked, soused and served with very subtle sauce – it was all a great treat.

Shortly before we left Germany we were invited to lunch with the head of the railways, who'd spent most of the war in Sweden. It was a delicious meal, and I can still remember the beautiful meat – so tender that I could cut it with the side of my fork – and the old-fashioned ice cream, in a tall column of pure cream flavoured and coloured most wonderfully. I have not had ice-cream as good as it since.

The Germans know all about good food, and therefore missed it dreadfully during the war years. They love to drink endless brandies at a party without any bad effect. For the Allies at the time all alcohol was very cheap, about 6 pence for a small whisky and 1 shilling for liquor. For most of us who had not seen these things for years, it did indeed add greatly to the pleasure of life. Looking back, one wonders if all those woods and mountains and lakes were really so beautiful; or was it just the wines we had for lunch that made us think so?

In the years following the war, both the Labour politician Ernest Bevin (who was Britain's Foreign Minister) and the Conservative politician Anthony Eden, came to the conclusion that the occupation of Germany as at first planned was far too long. As a result, it was speedily phased out, withdrawing the Control Commission. At the time I was very doubtful about the wisdom of this, and whether it would help or hinder Germany's recovery. But at the same time, I also knew, that because of the intricacies of German politics and the deceptions occurring in high places (some of which I've outlined in this chapter), the Germans were able to run rings around us. In other words, it was beyond the scope of officers on the Allied Control Commission to run the country.

Staying with the topic of Germans running rings around Allied occupiers, in 1945 a book was published called *Assize of Arms: The Disarmament of Germany and Her Rearmament (1919–1939)*. The book was written by Brigadier-General John Hartman Morgan, who'd served as Deputy Adjutant-General in Berlin from 1919 to 1923, as well as at the Inter-Allied Military Commission of Control. I did not come across this excellent book until after my four years in Germany from 1945 to 1949, and I'd left the country. Morgan's book was an in-depth account of the occupation after the first war 1914-1918. What fascinated me was that many of his findings were the exact same as my own. I just wish that everyone on the post-WW2 Control Commission (including 'yours truly') had been forced to read it at the time. Within less than 30 years, we were being fooled and deceived again by this formidable people.

I've already listed a few of some of the deceptions I discovered. But there were countless others. For example, in one locomotive shed I found a store of ball bearings sufficient for the entire Ruhr. In addition, I found that after making measurements and calculations on many of the busy lines in the Ruhr, most the rails were good for a further six years. Nevertheless, time and time again, requisitions would arrive in our office for thousands of tons of steel for rails. I was so staggered that I sent some of these reports to A. J. White of the Delaware and Lakwana Railway, who was the Marshal Aid representative for railways at the time. Like myself, he understood exactly what was occurring and such requisitions did not go through in our time.

On another occasion, while going over the Krupps' works with A.J. White – sorting out purely war materials for destruction – I noticed that at one side of a workshop there were certain cranes, which were not usually used in railway workshops. Instead, it was more usual to use gantries. As a result, I asked my interpreter to find out what had been built there. We were told that these cranes were used to build railway engines. Still incredulous, I asked my assistant to ask one of the workmen what had been built here, and the reply was that they had been used to build tank turrets.

General Morgan says in his book that 400 guns were built in Krupps between the end of the first war in 1918 and the signing of the 1919 Armistice. He also says that there were more guns and howitzers bricked into the walls of Konigsberg than the Germans had in 1914.

I had many meetings about over-expenditure of materials, and at these meetings I found the ordinary German engineer a very good type. The trouble (or deceptions) usually started when you encountered one of the autocratic-type fellows. I remember how I was once asked to address a meeting of railway officials in connection with my findings. After explaining what we had been doing, I declared, *"It is sad that you have not yet forgotten Hitler's instructions, and you are lying as fluently as he did."* This contentious address of mine was later circulated. At least they knew that I was aware of what was going on, and that I wasn't afraid to say so.

In the Essen area there was an enormous amount of work going on. To try keep a check on this, I devised a scheme whereby we had three copies of each plan, one on site, one they kept and one which I kept in my office. Upon completion, they would send in their copy of the plan to me for checking. In some cases, I had doubts about excessive expenditure on materials, and also, places being so-called 'inaccessible'. On my watch, such places were always visited and dug up for inspection. This probity and also having to send in a completion plan, made them very careful about wasting materials. I also had a graph system showing progress on work and expenditure, and at a glance we could see how things were shaping up. After my four eventful years in Germany on the Control Commission, I had to look around for another job.

Chapter 18

Railway location in Nigeria – floods, heat and insects from Nguru to Maiduguri and onwards to Bama

Getting back to London from Germany in 1949, I went along to the Crown Agents for the Colonies; because people were talking about development, and they suggested that I might like to work on a location for a possible railway line in Nigeria. I thought that this would be very interesting and arranged to come back again to discuss it. Anyway, when I next went to see them, they informed me that I would now have to go to the Colonial Development Corporation (C.D.C.), as they had handed this project over to them. I was sorry about this, but I went along to the C.D.C. office and we discussed this railway location in Nigeria.

I was surprised when they showed me aerial photographs taken of the district, with a certain amount of cloud, no ground connection, and on which they had marked where this railway line was supposed to be. Despite believing that the photographs were not much help, I nevertheless agreed to go out to Nigeria and make the survey. Basically, the object of the project was to find the best location for a track between Nguru and Maiduguri, and then on to Bama. It was a fair distance and most of the way was through bush country. There were three considerations foremost in my mind: first, avoiding marsh country; second, avoiding steep cuttings; and third, the need for large embankments. To fail to do so meant people working on the new line would succumb more easily to illness (both from heat and overwork). Please note, dear reader, that for the remainder of this chapter, I'm going to furnish details of when and where my work during 1950 in Nigeria took me, as well as what the work entailed, based on various written records from the time in my possession. To begin, on April 20th, 1950, I flew into Kano – a city *in northern Nigeria* and the capital of Kano State – with the flight out taking six and a half hours. Shortly after arriving, I went to see Khalil, one of the wealthiest Lebanese people in Kano. He informed me that he would get me a cook and servant through his 'boys'. In the meantime, I stayed in the Railway Rest House. Two days after my arrival I flew to the Nigerian capital Lagos to fully inform the Chief Engineer (C.E) of Nigerian Railways about my survey work. The C.E. was named Gahan and from the start I really liked him. He appeared to want to get on with the construction straight away, and totally agreed with me about avoiding unnecessary curves through the swamps, and that with good organisation we could do 4 miles of track laying a week.

After leaving Gahan, I then flew from Lagos back to Kano in a De Havilland Dove aircraft, flying at about 5000 feet most of the way. It was a lot quicker than the train, which took three days from Lagos. Back in Kano, my Lebanese contact Khalil had come up trumps and I engaged a cook called Lletulia and also a steward called Oomahoo, who did batman, washerman, etc.

As regards my work, since my plan was to initially have my main admin office in a place called Nguru, on April 29th I used motor transport to travel there. Unfortunately, the motor transport had insufficient spares, with the vehicle's tyre pressures all wrong, pumps useless and no pressure gauges. Despite all this, we reached Nguru by 6.30 pm, having motored all day, and having gotten stuck in the sand several times along the way. Upon arrival, we discovered we were short one theodolite and two levels, which had been put on the wrong boat from London. The country around Nguru was lovely and wild and I was very impressed by the cheerful natives, full of enthusiasm pushing cars and lorries when they got stuck in the sand. Believe it or not, the temperature that first night in Nguru was 110 degrees Fahrenheit (which is about 43 degrees Celsius). Indeed, parts of Nigeria were so hot at the time, that a lady named Gillian informed me it was 124 degrees at a nearby place a few days before, and it was still only April!

As regards the work itself, I had three work parties on the go. At the start I was kept very busy, especially as only one of our three work parties was fully equipped. As things transpired, the other necessary tapes and instruments and so on would not arrive until the second half of May. However, in the meantime I ensured to keep everyone busy. I remember one chap had a tough go of dysentery, and another nice young lad got too much sun.

By early May, our survey work so far had revealed that the railway route which looked so flat from the air, was unfortunately not as flat from the ground. Earlier, I got a very nice letter from the Chief engineer, and he totally agreed with me about my choice of location for the planned railway line.

Also, we discovered that the two rivers that flowed between the Gashua and Dampchi portions of the planned line were extremely dangerous. Consequently, we knew that it would take a lot of ingenuity, careful planning and expert topographical work to build a railway which would not be washed away in the floods – which occurred when those rivers overflowed. After much topographical work, we worked out that the best way of safeguarding any bridges was to place extra relief spans farther back from the main bridges.

By mid-May 1950, I had moved from my Railways Rest House accommodation into a nice little house with flyproof wiring, which thankfully was in good repair. On May 18th, just three days after the move-in, I left Nguru to travel to Gashua, which was 40 miles away as the crow flies. I was worried about that area and wanted to get it carefully mapped before the floods came and both the rivers in question rose. As I mentioned already, by now we had three work parties on the go and all of them were concentrating on survey work in this vitally important area, as our priority was not to let the coming rains defeat us. Once everything was in place and the rains came, we could watch the movement of the rivers and floods with reference to the 5 feet posts which we hoped to put in every 1000 feet. Although this concentration of work parties was not in accord with what London wanted, nevertheless I knew exactly what I was doing, since once a country is flooded, an exact topographical survey is almost impossible. I knew the big error on our part would be to underestimate this crucial flood zone between Gashua and Dapchi.

Also, during May 1950, I'm happy to say I was able to bring back a theodolite and other necessary instruments and things from Kaduna and Kano, so that now all our parties are properly equipped – apart from the instruments from London which had not yet arrived.

After a few days checking on work in the Gashua-Dapchi area, I next flew to Maiduguri on an ordinary Avro York aircraft, travelling at a height of about 20,000 feet. Upon arrival, I commandeered a Railways office there, which consisted of one typewriter and a clerk named Bruce. Although I had endless letters to answer, I knew they'd have to stay waiting on my desk, as an issue of alignment had cropped up surrounding one faulty survey done by a guy named Rice. In short, Rice had planned a portion of the line along a route with far too many curves, hugging a rotten road. I wasn't one bit happy and considered it grossly misaligned, and in need of rectification. As a result, I immediately cut out 4 of the 9 curves and then phoned to do a reconnaissance of the area in question, to try locate a 40-mile straight with no curves. I knew my policy of seeking straights would not only ensure a safer line, but it would also make savings of thousands of pounds.

So, the next day I headed to the bush on horse to check Rice's area for myself. After a few hours of riding, when I reached a place called Kwenawn, I poured masses of water over my head and face. It was not as easy as I initially thought to locate a straight of 20 miles plus through the country – some of which was quite prickly – as well as to have to take compass bearings with tired horses bothered by flies fidgeting in the background. However, nobody ever said the job was going to be easy! Eventually, I found what I wanted and saved ¾ mile in 8, which was a saving of about £6,000. As far as I was concerned, these were the crucial factors which would determine whether our survey succeeded or not.

Soon afterwards, we had a sandstorm which was so bad that I actually passed ¼ mile too far away from a village, because I did not see it. This meant that I rode about 26 miles instead of 20 miles.

A few days later I contacted London on my little radio and the line was perfect. I gave them the latest update on my 3 work parties as follows:

No.3 work party was near here in heavy wooded country, which was slowing them down.

No.2 work party are running into snakes.

As for No.1 work party, I planned to go to Maiduguri the next week to start them there, and then work back along the proposed route.

Two days later I went to Gashua to work with No.2 work party. A fellow called Nicholas was there all by himself and we cut through about two miles of country. We were laying out a fine bold line, completely ignoring the road and in the process saving miles of track and travelling time in the future. It is worth noting that at Gashua there was no telephone, posts were spasmodic, so I arranged a motor bicycle postal courier service. Also, where we were working near Gashua, we saw the most beautiful gazelle.

At the beginning of June, I went to Maiduguri to see how work was progressing there. As soon as I arrived, I called to see Humphrey, the senior person there, whose official title was Resident Officer. He and everyone else were most awfully nice and had reserved a semi-permanent house for my use, so I was able to have a bath without spiders and things in the water. Believe you me, this was absolute luxury!

A few weeks before that, an official at Kaduna called Sir Eric Thompston had advised me that the proposed line ought to go from Lentewa to Maiduguri. Anyway, I reported this to London, and they replied that I should have left the issue alone, since Rice and Woodward had agreed to go round Damatura. Well, as things eventually panned out, the Government wanted the line to go direct from Lentewa to Maiduguri, so, I was right all along.

Following this, over the next few days I spent much time riding all over the Maiduguri area to choose a site for our proposed railway station there. I also talked with several local notables about the proposed line.

As you may have guessed by now, having either a horse or horses and being a competent rider was absolutely vital to the work, since travel by horse was often the best way to get around the vast areas we were surveying. On behalf of the C.D.C., I had bought a pet of a horse, with a velvet mouth, from a vet named Walker. During that stint in Maiduguri, I rode that horse about 20 miles each day and he was a wonder! Our other horse was a big loose-limbed animal.

Also, around this time, I was asked by my superiors to do two extra surveys for the Nigerian Railways: the first of a possible Lentewa to Maiduguri route; and the second of a possible Lentewa to Tamatura route. Although I had no problem doing them, nevertheless these surveys delayed the completion of the entire project by about 2 months. My plan was to first run a trial line, and then an exact one. As I touched on already in this chapter, the most important thing for me was planning the most direct route possible, since it was usually the safest and cheapest. I estimated that a direct route would save at least ¼ of a million pounds, a figure not to be sneezed at! Also, at about this time I bought a ½ inch bore shotgun for £16, just in case it was required. I had no wish to shoot anything as majestic as an elephant or leopard, but I knew it might be well to have a gun, just in case some disgruntled wild animal did come at me.

On June 15th I journeyed to Bama and then onwards into French Cameroon, in order to do some reconnaissance of where the proposed line could run from Maiduguri, passing through Bama, and then onto Cameroon. I quickly mapped a route along a lovely high-rolling ridge, which was wide enough for a good alignment. By June 19th, 50% of our original survey work was successfully completed – and considering that the official measuring instruments for two of my work parties did not arrive until May 24th, this was not too bad, and I felt satisfied with our progress.

In early July I flew to Lagos on a De Havilland Dove aircraft, in order to brief my superiors about our work so far. We could not land at Jos because of heavy rains, and as a result, we went on to Kadua, and then flew from there to Lagos, arriving at 7 pm. It was quite rough, but the pilot made a very good landing. At the meeting, it was quickly discovered that nobody seemed to know where the French wanted the railway to enter the French Cameroons. Although I had done a preliminary reconnaissance, everything was still up in the air on that subject.

Also, everybody congratulated me on the speed of the surveying, and of course, Gahan the C. E. made it clear he trusted me absolutely and would not send anyone to check on my alignment.

As for Lagos, the natives there were a very mixed lot, and wore every kind of garment made of brightly patterned stuff. Also, they are very cheerful, with some of them honest and others less so. After Lagos I flew to Maiduguri, arriving back on July 6th. On July 12th I travelled to Gashua in a three-ton lorry, travelling 180 miles, as I wanted to start the trial borings for the planned bridges there. I took food and my camp kit, as one never knew how long these journeys might take, now that the rains had started. My bearer Oomahah (who was a good little fellow) accompanied me, and we also had a small tent and 8 gallons of water.

On July 17th I attended activities in Maiduguri celebrating the end of Ramadan. I attended a most spectacular display of horsemanship. The horses had collars of silver and every colour of gay trappings, and the riders had long spears (or swords) and went galloping madly past us spectators. It was all quite exhilaratingly spectacular! At one stage during the event the Chief Wazir and the Mukaddem advanced towards our officials – Humphreys and the D.O. – saluting them with their

155

ceremonial spears pointed downwards. I was only two seats away, so I had a good view. Then finally, the king of Bornu came along in his car, surrounded by horsemen, with some wearing chain mail. We might as well have been in another age. The old fellow even shook hands with me! I liked the Mukaddem's horse's face the best of the lot, even though there were some very fine horses, and some of the older men were riding absolutely perfectly.

Believe it or not, a few days later on July 23rd, after no less than 3 months of working, my kit eventually arrived safely at my residence in Maiduguri. It was marvellous once more, having my own saddle, breeches and boots. The very next day Monday July 24th, I left with about 15 men and three horses, with one of the men being an interpreter and the Shehir's representative. My plan was to spend a few days surveying country 5-miles on each side of a 293 degrees magnetic bearing. The country for 70 miles was completely unknown to any of us, and to our knowledge at least, had never been properly mapped. As I said, I rode on a bearing of 290 degrees using my small prismatic compass, and after 70 miles, when I touched in to a place on the map, I was correct to within a mile. This was not bad when one considers that about 60% of the country we traversed was heavy bush, and much of the time I could only see about 10 yards ahead.

The first day out, after about an hour, the rain started and increased to a torrential downpour lasting about four hours. As a result, all our clothes and bedding were wet through. Although the rain didn't penetrate the fibre suitcase, it nevertheless beat through the valise cover. Things got so bad, that after about two hours, our guide collapsed with fever, and we had to wait until we could get someone else. Either way, it eventually all worked out well, as I was able to get a clear picture of the country. However, a by-product of our adventures in the bush was that my face got rather sore from branches hitting it, as well as the sun burning it. As a result, it was very painful if I touched it in my sleep.

On one day during that particular trip, when approaching a rather ominous looking bit of country, I had the feeling that there might be wild buffalo about, even though I had been told there were none. When I sent for my gun, I discovered that the bearer was miles behind. So, I went on cautiously, and there directly in my path (about 100 yards away) was a huge buffalo. Needless to say, I made the widest detour possible around him. Other than that incident, I did not worry about wild animals on the trip. I saw wild hippo, more buffalo and lots of gazelle. Perhaps the worst day of all was when my shirt was torn to ribbons by the thorn.

Also, on that particular reconnaissance trip – which lasted over a week - there were millions of flies, except for two days when it was very hot. I did about 7 ½ hours riding daily, which was not bad. I also remember how one day during that trip, on our way to Lentewa, my interpreter went off privately, and after about ten minutes we shouted for him and got no reply. Hours later he reached camp, having gone off for 10 miles in the wrong direction. On yet another day, a local guide was taking me from one village to another, but after about 50 minutes, we were back at the same place we had started from. That's how easy it is to get lost in this terrain.

In August, we used our newly acquired Land Rover to do

more surveying work in the Gashua area. It took Java and me 10 ½ hours to cover approximately 100 miles, and along the way we passed endless lorries stuck in the mud. We even managed to get bogged down twice in the mud ourselves, and only with the help of about ten men were we able to extricate ourselves from it, after about an hour. Without the Land Rovers we could not travel after rain. Believe it or not we had three inches of it fall in one hour, and consequently the whole country was green and there were millions of mosquitos.

Also, during that month of August, we finished the 224 miles of surveying work to Nguru. Towards the end, we found it very tiring, not knowing if we would get through to our destination before nightfall – what with all that digging under the car, cutting brushwood and packing it in, to release us from muddy quagmires. The Rover behaved awfully well, and we travelled with a five-ton jack and palm tree logs, which helped greatly when we did get stuck.

Also, during August, I did much compass survey work to try and fix the correct position of Bama in relation to our station site at Maiduguri. The crops were so high that it was difficult riding to keep clear of the deep sands. Indeed, one day I nearly rode into quick-sand and would have lost my horse, but thankfully I managed to get him out with some help. The corn thereabouts was 12 feet high, so I had to take readings every 200 yards.

Now perhaps the big challenges I faced during all this period was London wanting things done one way and Railways wanting them done both another way and immediately. The problem I faced was I had not got enough staff to complete either option.

In September, our survey work continued as hard and relentless as ever. One of the major challenges we faced in that month was that where we were working had not experienced such heavy rains for 20 years, so many villages were flooded. For example, during our work on the Lake Chad route at the time, some roads were so flooded that not even the Land Rover could traverse them.

Also, in September I re-checked and rectified many of the levels, some of which were done in error by an incompetent person, who was duly sacked. Also in that month, I took an eventful journey to Gashua with my work colleague Koskas and a few others. The journey was much tougher than we thought it would be – 20 to 25 miles riding each day and wading through endless swamps is a lot! By the end of the month, we had finished the reconnaissance to Bama.

As it turned out, by October 1950, I'd completed the main survey I'd been contracted to do, as well as the various extras that had been asked for. So far there was no word on who the construction job of the proposed railway would go to, or when the construction would commence, even though I inwardly prayed and hoped we'd get it, as we had asked for the job.

Unfortunately, I was to learn over the next while that government policies change, and contracts can be broken. At this juncture, let me state that I love civil engineering, in particular big public works projects such as building bridges or railway lines. I genuinely think being a civil engineer is the best job in the world. But by their very nature, civil engineering projects often fail to get government approval or funding, due to a change of government policy or whatever, and so are scrapped. Governments change, and money which was perhaps initially earmarked for building bridges or railway lines or hospitals, may eventually get redirected to something completely different. In a nutshell, with civil or public works engineering, one always has to be prepared for bitter disappointment. With regard to the proposed railway line from Nguru to Maiduguiri (and on to Bama), my contract was terminated without any warning. Needless to say, it came as a great shock to me – so much so that I got a bout of paralytic malaria and had to be helped onto the plane at Kano. However, I soon recovered when I reached London.

It had been a tough assignment, with 'not much jam' (as they say), but I was proud of the prodigious work I had done. I had travelled thousands of miles in all sorts of conditions. I had also come up with many innovative solutions, such as making a plan for a more direct route, which I considered would save a lot of money. However, the reaction to my money-saving plan from head office in London was (believe it or not) a negative one – that I was *"Not to cut corners."*

At that time the C.D.C. had many vast schemes on the go: ground nuts, forestry, fish and various others. They also had some splendid people engaged in such schemes. However, for me the big spanner in the works was always theorists in London giving instructions to such 'splendid people' without any local knowledge, and totally disconnected from what was actually happening on the ground. As a result, such 'splendid people' were in effect forced out and had to find other employment. For example, a prime foolish instruction that sticks in my mind was London sending me out by air from England (at great expense) a measuring wheel, which was supposedly to be pushed over the survey line (in the same way that one might measure the distance of the Great North Road). However, to try do devil's advocate and see things from London's perspective, of course, there is often a difference of opinion between what the guy in the field thinks and what head office thinks. I remember how in one case the Chief Engineer of the Railways and the General Manager did not agree with the London office, and eventually the High Commissioner was dragged in to find a solution. However, that said, it always seemed to me that the man on the spot nearly always knows best.

Chapter 19

Italy, West Pakistan, and hydro-electric scheme for the Kafue Gorge in Northern Rhodesia

By May 1951 I was back in London looking for a job. By now I had had about 30 years Civil Engineering experience, and indeed I had some very nice testimonials from people I had worked for. Bill Lubbock had often said that I should try for the position of 'Agent' to a contractor, as he thought I was good with labour and that men liked working for me; so that when in 1951 I was offered a job with the Cementation Company I was delighted.

I was interviewed by a Mr. Grundy, their Chief Engineer. First, he looked through my records, and then giving me a few sheets of paper and a large office, he said, *"Now, Mr. Harpur, I want to know what you really do know."* I did wonder what was coming next, but then he just said simply, *"I want some estimates and working drawings for three tunnels – 10, 20 and 40 feet in diameter – into sand hills in Pakistan."*

It was quite a good exercise, and I never knew if he did really want these drawings for real, or just to test me. Given the technology available at the time, tunnelling was not easy, and tunnelling into sand was very difficult. I knew there were no books that could provide me the necessary information. This was simply an area of engineering that one had to learn from experience. Indeed, as I write this story, I don't think there is a book written yet which will tell you how to test a rivet properly!

Anyway, I got the tunnelling drawings ready, as well as doing various drawings for other projects. Also, I flew out to West Pakistan to see a dam and took a cross section and several photographs.

Another project I was involved with was the water supply for Karachi. Part of this was a big tunnelling job, and when I arrived by ordinary aircraft to Karachi, I went out straight away to look at this work. However, the next morning, due to extreme exhaustion from air-travel, I had forgotten most of my preliminary findings from the days before, so was unable to write up a report. As a result, I had to revisit the project that day. There's no doubt but these long flights from London to Karachi really tired one out.

I then returned back to London and did these working drawings. Dhow dam was a very interesting scheme because there was heavy flooding from the Baluchistan hills two or three times a year, and there was never any warning when those floods were coming. Although I planned to do the whole job by overhead cable, to avoid the floods, and to minimise the risk of losing our complete plant to the floods, nevertheless Mr. Grundy did not altogether agree.

My next assignment was a dam in the South of Italy. Mr. Neelands, the Company's chairman, wanted me to go there and make a report on the building of an earth dam, costing about £2 million. This was being done under the Marshall Aid Scheme, and the proposed dam was to be located about half-way between Naples and Bari, near a quaint place called Lavelle.

So shortly afterwards, I found myself at Lavelle, where there was only one house with a bathroom, and where all the houses seemed to be adorned with enormous plaster saints and crosses and lamps. As it turned out, the good lady who owned the house with the one bathroom was willing to take me as a lodger, so I got a room there. Unfortunately, she omitted to divulge to me that most of the village used this bathroom, not so much to bathe, but to wash their clothes, so the bath was usually full of washing!

My Italian was largely guesswork, as some words were similar to Portuguese, and the only thing I really knew in Italian were the numerals. As for Lavelle itself, it was the noisiest place I have ever lived. I always relished that too-brief interlude when the children stopped playing in the street, and the women stopped talking to each other across the street from balcony to balcony, and it was time to settle down for sleep. However, right on the bell at 5 am each morning, the local farmers with their mules and cracking whips would wake up the early morning cockerels, and the noisy day would begin again. Although my wife sent me ear plugs to help me catch some shut-eye, somehow they were either mislaid among the countless holy ornaments near my bed, or else someone (without asking me) had borrowed them on a long-term basis!

The dam was situated across an old valley – between

1500 and 2000 feet wide – composed of sand and silt. On one of my visits to Milan I had found the record of the trial borings, which showed nothing but silt, and I knew they intended building the dam with an open excavation method. I thought that this method would be dangerous across this valley, where there was only silt. Undoubtedly, there would have to be a lot of pumping, and this would certainly cause cavities, or boils under the floor of the dam. The danger was that the dam might be almost complete before these cavities would cause cracks through settlement. In many ways, building a dam is akin to playing chess – to be successful, one has to be able to plan and see several moves ahead. Put another way, one has to be able to *"see around corners"*, as the old saying goes.

Anyway, what occurred next was I had a meeting with Mr. Gammon, who was on the board of the company. It was a board meeting and at some juncture in it, I interrupted proceedings to tell them of my findings. I said, *"Gentlemen, I am very worried and very puzzled, because either you are not engineers, or you are not honest. I have seen from the accounts that you have undercut everyone by £200,000, claiming that you can build this dam by an open excavation method without the use of a cofferdam. In my opinion, this is a very dangerous type of construction."* Their reply staggered me: *"This is a cash cow we are going to milk."* I had a lot to learn about Marshall Aid.

When I told Mr. Neelands, he withdrew the company's security of £100,000 pounds, which had been offered to help with this work, as well as releasing me. So, I went home. When I returned from Italy, Mr. Grundy sent for me and this time he wanted working drawings and a full-scale estimate for the

Kafue hydro-electric scheme in Northern Rhodesia. By now I had an even larger office and got to work with enormous pleasure.

By the way, Sir William Halcrow and Partners were the consultants for the Kafue scheme, and their plan was to build a fairly low dam across the river; where the water would be taken through a tunnel and there would be a drop of 1000 feet, and then after about five miles there would be another drop of 1000 feet. This would give the required power for the scheme. I was alone on this project and had to contact all the firms concerned with it, the chief of these being Morrison-Knudson, a huge company which does work worth about £1 million a year. There were also several other firms involved, including John Laing Group and Metro-Vickers.

It was very interesting meeting these experienced people, and we discussed every angle of the construction. After about seven months' work, I arrived at the cost of £15 million. My labour ratio was one European to every ten Africans. Mr. Grundy thought it should be one to five, and this bumped up the cost by £2 million. By the way, when the Khariba dam was built during the 1950's by Impresit of Italy, it was done with a labour ratio of one Italian to every ten Africans.

Although the suggested method for this work was a coffer dam, I did not agree with this. The reason being the river had a rock bed, and there would be little penetration for the steel piling. In addition, we knew that in flood time big islands would float down and would soon distort the coffer dam. Even worse, such 'islands' could not be broken up and would be laden with crocodiles. In short, I felt using the cofferdam method was asking for trouble. Instead, my plan was to use timber flumes, which the water would pass for about nine months of the year, and so during this time the construction could proceed in safety. It's worth noting that a cofferdam on a rock bottom is most unsound, even when there are no floating islands or crocodiles.

If I remember correctly the tunnels were to have been 20 feet in diameter, and one of the major problems we faced was how to get to the bottom of these two 1000 feet drops; in particular, at the halfway point it would not be easy. Among other challenges, we would have to safely bring locomotives (of about 25 tons each) down the hillside, where the slope was about 1 in 3. To overcome this particular challenge, my plan was to put in twin tracks at about 6 feet apart, and then to sling the engine on a cradle. This manoeuvre would be controlled by an earth anchor and a hand winch. I had made good use of earth anchors in this way in Assam and in Iraq, when handling heavy girders and supporting derricks.

Everyone was rather surprised at this idea, but no one had a better suggestion, and I knew it was possible. However, Mr. Grundy was not altogether in agreement. Also, we found that the freightage rates to the various African ports varied enormously, so the question of shipment to East or West Africa or to Angola had to be worked out in great detail. In fact, I discovered it would be cheaper to fly in a D.H. bulldozer from London than to have a delay of half a day.

In the midst of all these big decisions, the whole scheme was sadly dropped in favour of the Khariba Dam, which I already mentioned. This came with the federation of the two

Rhodesias. As I touched on earlier, politics has a brutal way of grinding one's fondest civil engineering hopes to dust, and consequently many people were very sad.

Chapter 20

Glasgow Dock construction, and the B.T.H. Factory at Larne, Northern Ireland

After the Dam work was dropped, I was offered a job in Glasgow once again as an Agent to a contractor. So, I left London to look at the site and to find accommodation. At the time there was another job going on for the same company, and one day I went along to see that Agent. I found a very unhappy man, who pessimistically informed me he was the thirteenth Agent on that piece of work, and that he expected to get the sack any day soon. My appointment was for a dock extension at Shieldhall.

As far as I remember the monoliths were 36 feet by 36 feet and 48 feet deep. This was a very tricky job, even though we had what are called 'sand point wells', which provide a means of lowering the water level in the wet sand around the monolith. As it turned out, in this case I could only reduce the water level to about 8 inches below the final level of the monolith. This meant very careful sinking in case it would go too far, since friction in sand can be as high as 1000 pounds a square foot. We used Kentledge weights to counteract this. These monoliths were being built with shaped blocks, made on the site, and I had them painted on the outside to lessen the friction. This was not an unusual practice, and it was done in the construction of the Oakland San Francisco Bay caisson sinking, where the friction was reduced by 45% simply by painting the outside of the concrete with paint.

Although the contractor did not approve of my method, he nevertheless eagerly asked me to tell him all I knew about caisson sinking. Although I gave him six pages about caisson sinking, I did not mention what I thought would be obvious, which is that there must not be a great disparity between the water level inside the well and the outside water level. A disproportion of 10 inches could cause an upsurge or 'blow', which would shake the monolith and break it. My contract was terminated because they thought my methods were extravagant. However, it was a classic case of *"fools rush in..."* and all that, as shortly after I left an upsurge/blow occurred and the whole monolith had to be removed bit by bit.

By the way, from life experience, there are various ways of telling your friends that your contract has been terminated. You can fudge the issue by lying or you can simply say (as I did): *"I have got the sack."* I knew that in some cases (as here where the project faltered after you left) it is akin to a recommendation or plus in your resume, but it's hard for many non-civil engineering folks to understand this, and any termination is (in their eyes) an embarrassment. I suppose this is natural reaction for someone who goes to the same office – possibly in the same city – every day. They will never understand the fluid nature of employment in my profession.

Thankfully, we had kept on our flat in Chelsea, and after

another upheaval of moving all our baggage and furnishings from Glasgow back to it, we quickly settled back into life in London. In the meantime, I made my way down Victoria Street to tell some of my friends that I was looking for a job. Eager to find work, my first port of call was an old friend named Archie Hamilton, who I had befriended way back in 1923 in Diwaniyah, Iraq. He had done some splendid work there and I had been erecting his Callendar Hamilton bridges during the war. We had a lot to talk about, and he was really helpful and kind. By then I was over fifty and this was beginning to be thought of as too old. At the time I personally thought it was too old for some of the hot countries, and consequently I was hoping for something in the British Isles. After a few false starts, in March 1955 I was appointed Resident Engineer for the British Thompson Huston Co., who were building an enormous factory at Larne, Northern Ireland. This work would take about two years and would cost £8 million. It was still on the drawing board, with the Consultants being Sir Alexander Gibb and Mr. Paton (their partner).

After an interview with Mr. Paton in London, I then went up to B. T. H. office in Rugby and discussed terms of employment, as well as examining the plans. I also saw the results of the trial borings, which showed a perfect plateau on which to build a factory.

When I arrived at Larne, I saw them taking some small trial borings for an office or something, and what I saw 'in the field' did not fit in with what I had seen in the Rugby office. As a result, I felt that unless there was a geological fault there must be something wrong, and I was duly worried. When I told Mr. Paton of my anxiety, he agreed that we must take core borings in a grid fashion right across the site of the factory and the office, since this office alone was costing £250,000 (which was a hell of a lot of money).

For this work I contacted the Cementation Company because I knew they employed a firm called Thom, who were specialists in trial borings. They duly sent their rigs and took the bores with a diamond drill bringing up a solid cylinder of the stratus. After studying these and some careful levelling, we could see exactly what the foundations would have to be. The results also showed up the absolute fiction of the two previous bores, which were not within 50 feet of the actual levels finally reported.

Following these findings, I contacted Professor Charlesworth, who wrote *The Geology of Ireland: an Introduction*, and is a brilliant geologist. He studied the drawings and the detail of the trial bores, and then told me that the office position was 25 feet over the edge of the cliff. He further said that even though the field looked level, the rock below had begun to fall and there was a drop of 120 feet into the sea. What occurred next was our works manager Mr. Pedlar asked Professor Charlesworth to write a report about this for the Rugby Office, which he did (giving me a copy). I had some difficulty in making myself plain to the architects who wanted the office on the brink. However, Mr Pedlar realised that Professor Charlesworth knew what he was talking about, and we moved it in. Another consequence of our correct core borings was that the factory site had to have 1300 Franki Piles (which are high-capacity deep foundation elements) driven right across the position.

By the way, this was a very pleasant two years in the North of Ireland. Up to then, I had never been to this part of Ireland before and had only heard of Orange Parades and rude writings on walls. My niece Sally stayed with us there, and writing to a school friend on a post card she said, *"We have been to see the Orange Day Parade, and this is when the Protestants wear the kilt."* I thought her explanation was as good as anyone else's, and I could only laugh at the old bowler hats being worn well down on their ears, while their faces shone red and jovial, and not innocent of strong drink. The country was beautiful, and the coast road compared well with any place I had ever been. In addition, we made some good friends up there.

Construction of the B.T.H. factory at Larne, N. Ireland

Chapter 21

Joining British Railways, Kings Cross survey, and working on the new line to Bevercotes Colliery

I joined British Railways in 1957. After I had been with the Eastern Region for about a month, I was asked to do a rather difficult survey in the area of Kings Cross Station, going down to a depth of about 100 feet. The proposed survey would include the sub-ways and underground railways, spiral shafts, and all the other seen and unseen fabrications in the area. My assistant was a knowledgeable young man called Grant, who was an excellent draughtsman, and he and I had a small team of men to carry the instruments and assist in the work generally.

In a survey of this sort, one starts on the surface and measures a base line very accurately. Our base line was 320 feet along the in-coming taxi roadway. Starting with triangulation and having a base to work on, we then took two angles to fix the point of the apex of the triangle; from that we knew the sides and could build up three or four triangles off the one base. Needless to say, every measurement had to be spot on.

Before I started the survey, I felt it was important to have good instrument stations, and that these must be seen from three or four points. To mark these positions, I had small steel cylinders made, which were about a ½ inch in diameter and with a ½ inch hole in each. These were set in concrete in the pavements and in all sorts of places as I went along. Because, at the commencement of our surveying, I fixed points across the St. Pancras Road and in various places where the traffic during daytime is very dense, most of the survey consequently had to be done at night. In addition, I had excellent instruments, and my plan was that I would do the survey first, and then close it later on with levels (which would be an entirely different part of the work).

I began with triangulation and later on finished with a closing of what is called a 'closed traverse', which must be proved by the figures which go north and south, east and west, and come back exactly to where they started. The whole survey took about one year, and the closing error was never more than 1 ½ inches. All the figures were proved and could always be seen for the record.

I took measurements in some cases from the tube entrances and from the vertical shafts. In many cases these shafts were not used and had been closed for years. Indeed, in some cases the tunnels and tubes had last been used as air raid shelters. I distinctly remember there were some shafts which only measured 4 feet 6 inches in diameter. Some of the shafts were surrounding spiral stairways, and with the great depths, continuation of alignment was difficult.

I had special steel survey pins and the point of them fitted into the ¼ inch hole in the cylinder. Some were black and some white and I duly used them according to the light available. These pins were placed so that the centre line of the theodolite would be at the exact centre of the pin.

As well as the various subways I have mentioned, in our work we also had to contend with the Fleet Sewer and all the subsidiaries coming into it. I remember one very difficult one about 2 feet 6 inches wide and about the same height. In this I used a small radar box, and my assistant was able to trace my movements from the floor above. The reason I remember this so well is because I got a small cut on my hand, and this was thought to be very dangerous because of the nature of sewers. As a result, I was made to visit the doctor daily until every scratch had healed.

When we worked at nighttime, we put up what is called a 'Georges Cross', which was an illuminated signal on top of a tripod, and this tripod was exactly over the spot where the small cylinder was fixed. On one occasion after we had aligned everything with the greatest care (having examined the angle getting into position), upon turning to look around and then into the instrument, I saw that a motor car had (just a short while before) parked not four feet from the tripod. When I dashed over to move it, I soon found the car was already locked and the owner gone to Scotland on the night train.

I can also remember having great difficulty with one particular reading, which was on the surface, and I could not discover where my error was for about three days. After I did everything I knew to try and find out where I had made the mistake, suddenly I realised that there was a paving stone which was very slightly loose, and each time I leaned forward to take the reading, this stone would move slightly as I stepped on it, which was enough to alter the position of the instrument. As our work progressed, I got to realise just how important it was to be completely accurate – my credo being, one must be absolutely exact and the figures there for everyone to see.

I also remember Grant (who was a brilliant draughtsman), and me making our first plan. One component of it was a surface survey I did of an area taking in the Regent's Canal. This survey was detailed on a plastic sheet about 12 feet long, and it was not at all nice to work with. If I marked a spot with a needle point, it would close up so quickly that one had to mark the spot with a pencil circle. In addition, often the only way to find it again was with a magnifying glass. In a nutshell, it was hard work, and I was extremely glad when it was over. Working at night in London is only a little worse than trying to sleep by day.

It's worth noting that after we finished our surveying work, I was informed by the powers-that-be that it was very valuable, and I'm proud to say it was eventually used in the construction of the new Victoria line.

One other thing I remember is there was a lingering smell in the underground which permeated everything after a time, your clothes and person and whatnot! As our work turned from days to weeks and then to months, I began to think the smell would stay with me forever. Also, I think that perhaps one of the most tiresome parts of this work was having to wait until the electric current was cut off, so that we could step on to the track in safety. Some nights the cut off would only last for two hours, during which we would take our readings, and then we'd have to wait for the trains to start, before heading home to bed.

Also, in the tunnels there were 'refuges', so that men could get in to safety when a train was passing. To ensure our safety, one of the first things we did upon arriving at these tunnels was to locate exactly where these refuges were, since knowledge is power. After a diesel engine had gone through, the black smoke and oil fumes would hang about for a long time on still nights, and often make it impossible to find a place of safety. In the work I also learnt that railway men really love their work, and that although their work is interesting and exciting, nevertheless they're underpaid.

When the survey of Kings Cross was finished, I was sent to build the new train line to the Bevercotes Colliery located to the north of Ollerton in the county of Nottinghamshire. This showplace mine went into production in July 1965 and was one of the first fully automated mines in England. There were some deep cuttings and there were bridges over these cuttings, and here again I was faced with my usual problem: had the trial borings been correctly done? Prior to my arrival, all borings had been taken with an auger type bore. However, this does not give a very clear picture, particularly in sandstone. As these first results showed the sandstone to be absolutely sound, we went ahead with the bridges on what was supposed to be solid sandstone, for about five or six feet. In fact, we found it was not solid, and consequently we had to underpin these bridges, which was a costly job.

As Resident Engineer, my work approach was always, if one did not agree with the plan or had doubts about trial borings, then one had a duty to say so; since the Resident Engineer was ultimately responsible for the project, and a 'Yes' man was quite useless. Of course, there was always the chance that no one would listen to you, and this could be an absolute heartache, but at least you knew you'd done the ethical thing. That's what occurred in this instance, I gave my honest opinion to the powers-that-be (that the trial borings weren't good enough), but my superiors failed to listen to me. The end result was valuable taxpayers' money was wasted. The new line at Bevercotes was 4 ½ miles long, and to my knowledge it was the first new railway in England for about 50 years. It included a tunnel (about 1000 feet in length), 10 or 12 small bridges, and some of the embankment was 40-feet high; all of which called for much railway engineering experience.

Regarding the embankment, I distinctly remember how one contractor was rushing in soil and not compacting it as it came. He actually brought in 20 or 30 loads and just emptied it, without any spreading or compacting whatsoever. When I saw this, I immediately stopped the job and made him clear back the flattened surface to expose the stratum of loose soil; loose soil on a railway embankment can cause a dangerous settlement later. Although the contractor in question was furious and put in a claim against me personally of £930 for delaying the work, nevertheless the chief engineer agreed with me, saying I was absolutely correct in taking such a strong line. Eventually the claim was dropped. I was lucky in this job in that our work team was a tight one and we all worked well together. On the job we used 'walkie-talkie' radios to communicate over the wide area of our work.

I did several other jobs for the railways before I retired,

and one of the most extraordinary was at King's Cross, London. For this my bosses asked me to go through the old railways plans and destroy as many as possible, only keeping those which might be of some importance in later works. When I entered the building containing the old plans, my jaw just dropped. I had never seen anything like it. There were thousands of plans going back to the early days of building the railways. All these old plans were housed in an enormous plan-room and there was no more room for the new plans coming in. Believe it or not, perhaps the most difficult part was opening them and making them lie flat. We used heavy weights to do this. I remember some of these old plans were very beautiful, and must have taken many hours or even weeks to draw. The detail was amazing, and in some cases I can remember that the sunlight on each slate on the roof would be drawn in.

I think I went through about 100,000 and destroyed about 40%, keeping all completion plans and all drawings which showed buildings underground. As this was an old-fashioned plan-room with overhead heating, one's feet were always frozen on the stone floor. Most of the plans were on fine linen, and as they were being destroyed, I brought a few home to my wife. She thought she could make some sort of lining out of the fine linen, but even with hours of washing there was always a faint outline of some drawing showing through.

Around the same time I was sorting through those old plans, The Transport Act of 1962 dissolved the British Transport Commission (BTC), which up to then had overseen the railways, canals and road freight transport. In its place, it established the British Railways Board, which took over on 1 January 1963. The first chairman of that Board was Dr. Beeching, who made many changes. Over a number of years, he ear-marked many railway lines for closure.

When I joined the railways, many of the older people thought there would be work for years to come for men with railway experience, but the Beeching axe fell hard on the entire railways system – over 4000 route miles were closed, hundreds of stations were closed, and also there was the loss of thousands of jobs. Also, countless people without a car in rural areas – who depended on the railways – were basically abandoned. In the meantime, the roads were becoming more congested daily. In my opinion, much of the Beeching closures lacked foresight and it was hard to see the sense of it all.

If my memory serves me correct, in around 1967 I reached retirement age and I said 'goodbye' to what had been a very interesting ten years working for British Railways.

Chapter 22

Retire to Ireland, build in West Cork, employment on water supply schemes, and return to Castletownbere after 55 years

We were still residing in our London house when I started to draw the old age pension, and we soon realised we could not afford to live there. It was my wife who came up with a possible solution to this – she began researching stone cottages in the west of Ireland which would cost a few hundred pounds, and then be made comfortable with a few more pounds. As a result, she arranged that we'd travel to the west of Ireland to check various cottages out.

The papers said something about floods in certain parts of Ireland, so we telephoned to an Irish friend in London who said simply that, *"Cork was always under water after heavy rain."* Even now I do not know what she meant, because I have seen the heaviest rain pouring down for days and I have not yet seen the portion of County Cork we now reside in flooded. Anyway, I thought it was better for me to go and see for myself about these rains. So, I flew over and stayed at a very comfortable hotel called the 'East End Schull', where if the Gulf stream no longer warmed the coastline, at least the modern necessity of central heating warmed the hotel bedrooms – no more cold damp beds!

I was taken to see various old cottages by a very kind person who certainly had a lot more imagination than I had, since he could see all sorts of possibilities, that for the life of me, I could not imagine in my wildest dreams. I must admit that I have never really liked tiny rooms and low beams, so eventually when I was shown a two-acre site for a possible house, I knew I had hit paydirt, since we could build our own house on the site to suit our own needs. I duly telephoned my wife and told her that I had been shown the most beautiful place I had ever seen, overlooking a little harbour where there were two swans, *"just like the pond at Barnes,"* in our house in London which we overlooked.

I went again to see the two acre site and climbed in over a wall which fell down when I sat on it – the sun shone, the sea was a marvellous blue, the islands in the distance had clumps of golden gorse, and the air was like a garden of Eden; only I did happen to know that the air in Garden of Eden was in reality extremely hot and not very bracing.

I felt marvellous and took a photo of this paradise, which was only missing a house for us to live in. After that, I saw a solicitor, set all the formalities in motion and then went back to London to tell my wife. While she was thrilled and wondered how we could afford to do it, my bank manager was not at all thrilled. At any rate, we decided to make a clean break and sell the London house. It sold almost before the ink was dry, as several people made instant offers at the house agents. We were delighted with our price, as it would be enough to build the house we wanted on the two-acre County Cork site. But first, I had to take my wife over and show it to her. So, we arrived late one dreary evening into Schull, very tired after a long drive from Dublin. After dinner at the hotel, we drove out to see our field and I felt very anxious about what I had done, had I actually made a mistake? We spoke to Neil Cotter, who would be our nearest neighbour, and he kindly let us into his lane to inspect our property; it was chill and colourless. My wife and her aunt who had come with us both said we would feel better in the morning, and that just now we should go back to our beds in the hotel.

In the morning, we returned and it looked miraculous. The meadow was full of wild flowers, and the little harbour was just as beautiful as I had remembered. We plotted the position for our house with rocks from the wall, and although all was well, we knew that lots of hard work lay ahead. The house was eventually built by Barney Heron of Dublin, to a plan we gave them. It was a wooden house with a Cedar shingle roof, otherwise not unlike the Colt houses. I had first viewed the two-acre site in February, and we moved into our newly built house on it in the autumn. I planted about two hundred young trees and nearly one thousand bulbs. I learned to use a scythe and a pick. In fact, I had to dig each bit of the ground with the aid of a pick or crowbar, as it was very hard and had not been tilled for years.

Retirement was full of hard labour, but we loved it and when I brought the car home full of rhododendrons, it did not take much to imagine how beautiful it would be in the spring. In fact, the wildflowers were perhaps the most beautiful fauna of all to grace the area. I had various hobbies lined up to pass the time, so that it was a very great surprise when an engineer friend telephoned to ask if I would consider doing a small job for the consultant who was planning a sewerage scheme for a small village nearby. I said I would love to do it in my own time, as I had various commitments in my house and could only give a few hours weekly.

What happened next was I went to see the consultant, listened to what he had to say, and agreed to get involved. It would be interesting, and I had never worked in such a beautiful place before. Also, the drive each way was stunning. Before my work with that consultant finished, I was asked by Cork County Council would I mind overseeing a water supply scheme for another small place. This particular scheme included a little dam up on the mountain and 2 miles of pipes to the village. Although the job involved the simplest form of levelling, nevertheless I knew extreme care had to be taken with the water levels, since the latter would determine whether or not it was a success or a failure. After I successfully completed that job, I was greatly surprised to be asked if I would look after the water supply scheme for (of all places) Castletownbere – where I'd spend the first part of my army training many decades before. Bere Island was the place where my life as a soldier had begun and, to be honest, although one side of me remembered it with loneliness and bitterness – nevertheless another side of me also remembered how beautiful the whole of Bantry Bay really was.

The water scheme plan entailed the water being piped nine miles from lake Glen Beg to a reservoir above the town. Luckily, I had some of the best men I have ever worked alongside: friendly, polite, honest and keen to get the job done correctly. The major challenge with the job was successfully laying pipes in all the undeveloped extremes – from rocks and bogs to hills and plains, to floods and droughts.

Life in County Cork was very pleasant, the people were very friendly and very kind. Some of the neighbours helped us with the garden, and painting the house, and this is where Connie Griffin came in. I think he was about eighteen when we first knew him. He was always great for a laugh and always ready to help with any job (no matter how awkward). One couldn't have asked for a better neighbour. I remember he chose a good day to paint our chimney, when he could look over to the south and see Cape Clear eleven miles away. He played a big part in our lives over the years, while he was studying for the priesthood.

Also among our friends was Father Jerome Kelley who wrote *Seven Year Island*. Having read his book, I was so charmed by it that at Christmas I gave it to several people. The book offers a lovely description of those islands to the west of Ireland and the simple wisdom of their people.

Another milestone in our time in Cork was discovering a very tiny church called Altar Church, built during the famine with money collected by the rector to give employment as famine relief. The church lies among the hills and heather, in a bend of the road where the sea comes into the rocky bay – with the surrounding coastline adorned in gorse and primroses, honeysuckle and wild roses in the hedges, and foxgloves and bluebells doing their level best to survive the many Atlantic storms. On Sunday mornings, a long line of cars can be seen parking near the church, as it fills up. During the summer, tourists and visitors to the area swell the usual congregation of farmers and retired people (such as ourselves), who have come to live in the neighbourhood. Canon Christopher Hilliard is the Rector and he and his wife had been in India for years as missionaries. They knew many of the places I had been to, and we discussed many of the world's problems. My wife and I felt it was a real blessing to discover this simple low church Irish-Anglican service. Attending the service each week, I soon discovered that our rector Canon Hilliard loved reading from the Old Testament – bringing alive all those exciting ancient stories of battle – and I'm happy to say that after hearing him preach, David and Goliath took on a new importance for me. The little church is heated with oil heaters, and when we first arrived and saw the flame rising above the metalwork, and that no-one was alarmed, we felt horribly suburban.

The Hilliards became great friends: their kindness was beyond belief. They shared their garden produce with everyone, although I suspect we were high on the list as our garden was still part of the field and the gales swept over the patch taking the peas and beans with it. In contrast, their Rectory Garden is old and located in an old quarry, so that there is shelter and some of the best vegetables I have ever eaten come from it.

Here was this friendly greeting, and in a strange way this place was a little bit like the old church and Rectory at Timahoe in County Laois, where I first started my life. So, in a way, retiring to that part of West Cork was like coming home at last.

Personal Account by Daphne Harpur

My husband Ernest died in 1975. Although some family and some friends read his memoirs shortly after his death, it was our niece Sally who – after reading them one night – insisted that I write something from a personal perspective about Ernest, so that future generations would have some idea of his love for his engineering work and his zest for life.

Before continuing, I might as well say there were many times when life was challenging for us. But that said, he had such a wonderful sense of humour and tremendous kindliness, that when things were difficult, he would be marvelously optimistic. Also, he always or nearly always liked most people when he met them, and if I felt doubtful about someone, he would say I had a chess mind, this despite the fact he himself couldn't play chess. When I once tried teaching him the game, we ended up playing draughts, moving the pawns around the board and this he always won. I think a game had to have movement and be amusing in the funny sense for him to enjoy. Chess and golf were, he felt, just too serious, with little room for fun. In contrast, he would laugh loudly having swiped a tennis ball down the sideline, and he enjoyed the action of squash.

While he liked to win, he hated beating people, so he was actually not terribly good at winning. Although he won a few races sailing in a nice yacht on the Baldeney sea in Germany when he was at Essen, nevertheless, he did not really like racing and could usually be seen skirting the lake trying out manoeuvres on his own.

He was a very fit person and would always walk the longest way. Indeed, some of his friends called him 'Supra', meaning someone who was tough or gritty. However, in my opinion, this was far from reality because he was not tough (in the John Wayne gunslinger sense), but instead awfully couth and kind, and would go to endless trouble to help someone. I often remember saying to him, *"Why on earth did you go off there or do that or whatever?"* He'd reply, *"Oh the poor fellow, I felt sorry for him."* Whenever there was a visit to pay, he would think up something that might not be available in that place he was going to, and then take along a supply of whatever it was. As a result, there was always fish in the car when he returned back from Castletown Bere, and he would duly give our neighbours little presents of herrings, sole or cod which we couldn't get in Schull.

Often after he returned home from working abroad, I almost feared what would come out of his suitcases: all sorts of presents like lace and silk from India, oranges and mangoes from the Gulf of Israel, scent from Paris and many more exotic items. I can still remember well the lovely smell of that Parisian scent, because the daily help I had thought she would also like a little, and accidentally broke the bottle of 'Fleur de Rocaille' (at which I nearly wept). On one occasion he sent a packet of skins to make a fur coat – they were beautiful strong 'Marten' skins – but when they arrived my mother-in-law did not like the smell and had them buried in the garden!

So much of his life and travels were during times of rationing and shortage, so that he was always laden with what he felt was in short supply. He loved giving presents and would arrive laughing with something unusual. For example, he once bought me a dress length of black velvet when he had gone to Baghdad to work. At the time, it was too hot for me to travel out and it made a lovely dress for the winter. When I had worn it several times, he said one day, *"That dress always reminds me of the train at Hilla, because I had bought the velvet for you, and it was so hot, and you cried."*

Ernest had a strong feeling that a man was good because of what was in his heart, not what he professed. In other words, it didn't matter whether a man was a Hindu, Mohammedan, Christian or whatever, what mattered was how the man lived his life, and did he do good unto others. We often argued about this, especially when I would say, *"But he is not a Christian"*. Ernest would be quite hurt for his friend, whatever the man's faith.

As a child he had the normal religious education with perhaps a bit more being a parson's son. Since he left the army, he had lived in remote places, where the nearest church was often a hundred miles away, so it would be quite common for him not to get to a church. Indeed, for many periods in his life, he would only get to a church if he happened to be in a town on a Sunday. Once he said to me that he wanted a new bible, so I gave him a nice new Scofield Bible, and he read it from start to finish in about a month – not making much of the Scofield notes, but really enjoying those thrilling Old Testament stories – above all Proverbs! Many of these he knew because they were quoted in the Rectory in his youth, but some were quite new to him, and he loved them and would quote them to me: *"Better a crust where love is than a bouquet with strife."*

He also loved the story of David killing Goliath with his sling of stones. I don't think such stories had a major religious meaning for him. Instead he loved them for their adventure, and they were especially significant for him because of his travels to Babylon, Kish and Ur of the Chaldees, as well as Damascus and various places in Syria and Palestine.

His favourite part in the Bible was Corinthians 1, Chapter 13. When his mother died, he was in Italy, and in his absence, I was given a little book (which had been her bedside book) called *The Greatest Thing in the World* by Henry Drummond. In the book Drummond suggested reading the thirteenth chapter of first Corinthians every day for a month. Because it had been his mother's book, Ernest read it, and it revealed a whole new meaning of life to him, making sense of the Christian Faith for him. As I touched on already, through his life-experience he had known men from all sorts of backgrounds who had been wonderful, kind and brave, and here at last was the Bible confirming his inner belief: *"If one did not have charity and kindness at heart, then Christian teaching meant nothing."*

Also, Ernest always loved to talk with me about his engineering work, and explained in great detail some of the many challenges he faced in it. Despite the fact I could barely add 2 plus 2, ever the optimist, he would persist in trying to explain to me the intricacies of the strong lining of curves; how railway engineers worked to make the track curve 'gradual', undertaking endless little mathematical calculations to find the best approach. At least if I never got to understand what it all meant, nonetheless he successfully taught the method to several railway men, so that the running would be smooth. Indeed, in his pocketbook there was a diagram describing this method.

I also remember that he would often waken during the night with a shout, and then would say, *"I am so sorry, but I was dreaming that an elephant got in the house, or a tiger was trying to take you away."* He loved wild animals and read a lot of animal books, including all the Jim Corbett stories of man-eaters.

Another character trait of Ernest – he was utterly honest and would have revealed his last shilling to the smartest man. Because I am not so honest, I often felt furious when he produced a small amount to me, saying apologetically, *"The man I gave money to on the street asked me if I had anything else, so of course I told him I had."*

We did not have children and our friends often felt sorry for us, but actually it was a very mild disappointment for us. I remember the fear of having a baby during the summer in Iraq, which would have meant my returning home for several months; this was not what we wanted. Then when we got to Brazil, having a child would mean it would become a Brazilian and a son would have to serve in the forces there, all of which was not to our way of thinking. A great friend once said to us, *"You should have a son to die for his country."* We were outraged and replied, *"That is the last thing we want."* We could do with a son to live for his country, but that is as far as we wanted it. Anyway, it was a ridiculous sort of argument from a fellow who had no children himself.

Also, Ernest liked things to be done in good taste and he had some definite ideas about this. On this front, I am afraid I was a bit lax. One of his absolutes was punctuality and his whole day was ruined if I, or someone else, was late. He himself was never late for an appointment.

It is not always easy to live with someone whose standards are absolutely and completely uncompromising, and whose integrity was plain to see. But in these current times we live through – when standards are not too high – Ernest really could never understand why others did not share some of his ideals and standards, and he would feel outraged.

Another aspect of my husband's character is he did not fit in with big business, and when a firm was trying to make money by cutting costs and using poor materials, he would fight every inch of the way to keep standards at a premium, sometimes putting himself out of a job. After this scenario, I would say, *"Please try not to see if the concrete is too wet or if the trial borings are not the best possible,"* when he was discussing a contract. He would look at me as if I had stolen someone's purse and say, *"But don't you realise I am responsible for the specifications stating clearly how the job is to be done."*

Another absolute of his was answering letters, since he

answered all letters punctiliously, whereas I often did not. Also, if books were lost or borrowed, oh dear! When we jointly took out books from the library, often he would return them too soon, before I'd had a chance to read them, since I am such a slow reader. If he lent a book to someone else and it had not been returned after a suitable time, the book would be called for or he would send a note reminding the person. He simply loved books and read widely, and when he was working hard, he would read thrillers; but when things were less pressing, he read more serious autobiographies or travel history.

Though he was wonderfully healthy himself, he was terribly kind to sick people and would assure them that they would be well in a day or two. I think he said a little prayer as he visited people in hospital, but in fact he never stayed too long with them. I often felt he might have stayed longer, and I would say so, but Ernest felt, particularly in Ireland and Brazil, that he was delaying a person who wanted to get well and get back to his job. This in fact was the last thing they wanted, and often they would stand for hours talking to others but not to Ernest.

I remember how once his cousin Muriel came to visit us when they were both aged about 70, and when Ernest took Muriel a cup of tea in the early morning and said good morning, he added, *"Gosh, there is a pool of water under your bed."* The poor woman was horrified and said it could not be, and he waited a moment while she leaned out of her bed to see and then he said, *"April fool!"* Following that, he came back to me laughing and saying, *"Poor Muriel, I gave her an awful fright."* April 1st was always a day that made me feel like a hen barely holding on to all its feathers, or perhaps just its legs. I was always caught in the end.

For much of my life I was quite resigned to being some sort of widow. A grass widow was quite a common term. but there were many more: a sailing widow, pip stick widow, polo widow, shooting widow and so on. They all came my way, so I am not too astonished at now (after Ernest's passing) being alone.

There was a strange childishness about Ernest, in spite of all the ups and downs of his life, and in a wonderful way he never lost it. There were many occasions when I found it quite maddening, and when some fine philosophy I had thought about for hours or days was reduced to absurdity in a flash of youthful humour. I often felt hurt and wounded, but on reflection I feel it was probably good for me. Now that he is not here, I can get away with it, but I can still see the ridiculous, as he would have seen it, and it helps me to laugh instead of cry.

In his story there are many anecdotes which I wondered if it would have been better not included, because without his physical charm and his infectious laughter and sense of fun, they lose so much of their meaning. If he had had sons, then no doubt they may have squashed this sense of the ridiculous, but it was always interesting to see other people's sons listening intently to his stories of travel and encounters; and it could be that we lose much in the way the young silence themselves.

This incident of the Brahmaputra bridge had an

enormous effect on Ernest, and he talked about it for years; the whole river and the water courses of that Assam area persuaded him of the need to control those waters. When he read of floods and droughts in India and Pakistan, he was more convinced than ever that this could be prevented by controlling these rivers, in particular the Brahmaputra. I believe that he would have wished more than anything to have worked out a plan to control this huge river. His idea was that with all the money spent year after year dealing with these disasters, he could devise a scheme for tunnelling through the mountains by the upper reaches of the river, and then taking off channels of water. This water would then be used either to irrigate or feed hydroelectric schemes for India and Pakistan. Of course, it would cost millions and millions, but so does the annual disaster. He wrote letters to newspapers and talked to all sorts of people about this, but sadly no one was sufficiently interested to do anything about it. In this regard, I always wondered if he had special knowledge, because of his time in Assam and Burma. He thought that if a series of tunnels were built at intervals of 100 miles to control the flood water, then it would change the face of that continent from poverty to prosperity and plenty for all.

Also, ever since my husband was first in India, he had remembered the Himalayas, and he had always said that one day he would take me to see these marvellous mountains. But unfortunately, when he went again, he could not take me.

Now I just mentioned how he wrote letters to newspapers about flooding and the Brahmaputra. Another topic he had strong views about was the re-settlement of the Arab refugees. In September 1972, there was a letter in *The*

Times about this topic which interested him, and to which he replied. Although his letter was never published by the newspaper, I am giving it in full below, since it demonstrates how Ernest was always concerned about solving problems, in particular finding practical solutions which improved the quality of people's lives. Here's the letter:

Dear Sir,

In Mrs. Daniel's letter to you of Sept 20th, 1972, she suggests that the Palestine Refugees should be absorbed and resettled by their Arab brothers, particularly those of the rich oil states. How can we persuade these rich Arab nations to finance the reclamation of the Sahara, possibly assisted by Israel and Britain?

The reclamation of 2 million square miles of the Sahara is not impossible, using an underground sea called the Savourin Sea which is equivalent to the size of France, with 400 billion cubic feet of water and equal to the flow of the Rhine for 190 years.

All this is fully mentioned by Richard St. Barbe Baker in his book *Sahara Conquest*.

Having lived for fifteen years among Arab tribesmen, I feel very strongly for these unhappy refugees, and with so much money available they should be given a chance to develop that part of the world.

Yours,
Colonel Ernest Harpur,
Schull, West Cork. Ireland.

That was the letter Ernest penned to *The Times* in 1972. Staying with the topic of letters, his letters to me from Nigeria in 1950 were really very worrying, as I could see that all the time, he was trying not to make me anxious. At the time I felt he had really had enough hardship, and as he was 51 it could not be good for him. Also, I think the pay was very poor and too much was expected of these men in those awful conditions. When he eventually got home, he was awfully disappointed that the construction of the railway line was seemingly being shelved, and that he had to find another job. At this juncture I begged him to stay at home, since up to then he had always been abroad. Let me tell you, this was not so easy, as he was wonderfully fit in spite of all the travails of his work in the Nigerian bush! As for me, I felt I had had enough of this sort of life. It was time for us to settle down.

Once I can remember going to London airport to meet him in my mother's car, and as I stood watching the plane circling the airstrip, the chauffeur said casually, *"This is the sort of time these planes burst into flames."* I don't think he intended to upset me, but I have never forgotten it. When Ernest actually got off the plane looking very well, I could hardly believe it.

I think one of the most difficult things about the letters from Africa was telling people where he was and what he was doing, as it sounded quite extraordinary – all the places were remote. I was living in London and meeting friends and relations who were mostly working in London offices, and when they enquired about him, my answers usually went something like: *"Oh, he has flown down to Lagos and got back safely and rode 25 miles through jungle country. Oh, and yes, he saw buffalo and ate 30 mangoes. He has no mirror and there are no tables in his room. Also, his trunk took 3 months to arrive."*

197

As already mentioned, his surveying work in Nigeria took huge effort and stamina, and I've no doubt that for him it was like being back at war – living life in extremis! Then abruptly in the end, with no explanation at all, his Nigerian contract was stopped. So, I imagine that by then Nigeria Independence had been planned and someone knew that no money would be spent on new Railway lines or anything else. That's my own guess as to why perhaps the entire project was shelved, even though we'll never fully know. But on the human level, it was very frustrating for hardworking people like Ernest, committed to their work. After that, he wiped the dust of that job from his feet and became immediately interested in the next one, since he was an optimist through and through.

As regards my in-laws, the Harpurs were a happy family and the Rectory was a welcoming place where people came with their joys and sorrows: tennis in summer, social dances in the parish and bridge with the neighbours. The neighbours indeed were often miles away and the journey was made in a high trap. It was 8 miles to the station or the tennis club and even the 3 churches were about 4 miles apart.

I remember the Rectory where Ernest grew up had a small conservatory at the front door, with rooms on both sides of the hall, and leading to a back hall where the stairs went up to the bedrooms and a bathroom. The bath was a flat tin bath or a high bath, both of which could be taken into the bathroom if there was a fire, and the weather was cold. Also, in front of the house the lawn sloped away to some trees and a pond, and this pond provided extra water for the house.

I also remember there were two maids who did most of

the work, part of which was milking one or two cows and making butter. The dairy was an outside room and large pans of milk stood on shelves waiting to be skimmed with a saucer or large spoon. The cream was collected in a large earthenware crock until ready for churning in a wooden barrel churn. In addition, all the washing was done at home, long lines of clothes would hang in the field at the back of the garden, and ironing on a table in the kitchen was almost a daily routine.

The maids wore gingham dresses, aprons and caps, and after midday the gingham would change to a black dress with a white frill apron for afternoon tea times. A speciality of Timahoe Rectory was a Sally Lunn, which was a sort of sponge cake well soaked in melting butter. Sometimes tea was taken to a cave in the garden which was a popular hideout for the family. At that time the maids were Roman Catholic, and they were always anxious about living and working in a Protestant Rectory and consequently would say special prayers and sprinkle holy water in their rooms.

When war came in 1916 and the Irish Rebellion cast a shadow over all normal life, even quaint Timahoe Rectory was never the same again. Not that the Rebellion was felt at Timahoe, but very sad things happened in the wider area and beyond. Near to the Rectory lived the O'Higgins family and they were friends of the Harpurs. Doctor O'Higgins was the family doctor and a very well-respected neighbour. Sadly, In February 1923 he was shot by Anti-treaty Republicans during the Irish Civil War, which lasted from June 1922 to May 1923. His son Kevin O'Higgins, who was Minister for Justice of the Irish state, was himself shot dead by Irish Republican extremists in 1927.

My father-in-law, George, was a very kind person and he would always listen intently to the tales of sorrow which some parishioners would relate, and if he could, he would help them, often going out of his way to do so. Some years after he died, a family he had lent money to when they were in some difficulty, paid back the loan with interest. Some of the Harpur family know of the loan and it was quite large, indeed large enough to buy a small farm at the time.

As I mentioned earlier, Ernest loved nothing better than talking about his engineering work. Thankfully, I made a good listener, so that he wrote to me almost daily whenever he was away. During the war years when his letters came in packets of three or four after a week or two, it was not easy to get the story of what he was doing, particularly as he was not really allowed to tell anyone. Also, there was another hazard to all this, which was that I was working in Censorship, and I was often too tired to enjoy particularly those little miracle photo slides which he sent me. The details in them were so small, that I could sometimes only view them with a magnifying glass.

He wrote this book for his good friends. There were many whose lives had been influenced by him, and he wanted every nice young man to build something, particularly a bridge. He had a very strong feeling for his engineering profession, and as most of his forebears had been to university, he was envious of the ease with which young men nowadays can enter – as it had not been possible for him. This was a traditional thing and his father had written in his will that he hoped his sons would take degrees and do some service to the Community.

When I first got to Iraq after our marriage and went up by train to my new home at Quaraghan, it was all very strange and there was not a woman of any kind in sight. We had rather dignified Arab servants and an Indian cook, and there was a separate cook house with an oil cooking stove in a very small space. More than anything else, lots of men was my impression.

I was told not to go near the kitchen until I had been in the country much longer. The food was awful, and so very different to the food I was accustomed to. I remember the cook went to endless trouble to make me one of his masterpieces, which was a toffee basket full of fruit salad. He would bake the basket with milk strands of toffee, and I am sure it took hours, but it was not very nice.

We often had partridges and they would be accompanied by all the proper sauces, but carrots and beautiful roast potatoes were made into a kind of fluffy mashed puree. I cannot remember what vegetables we ate – they were strange foreign ones. Some were very nice, and 'ladies' fingers' were a rather sticky pod full of small peas. There were also fields of tomatoes and cucumber and melons, but even they had to be washed and all the water had to be boiled, and so too had the milk (which was buffalo milk). My recollection is this milk was not very different from normal Irish cows' milk.

Our bungalow was facing across the river and there were lots of turtles in the banks, with some of them about two feet across the shell. They were of all sizes, with some not bigger than a saucer, and they would try and slip into the water if we were near.

I also recall how Ernest would go out very early at about 6 o'clock in the morning, inspect the work on the bridge, and then come back and tell me what was going on. I did not understand at all, but he liked to tell me. There were small horses which they rode when they went to work. Ernest rode very well and was very anxious that I should ride, but I was very bad and really very frightened, and this was not made any easier by being informed: *"What the horses need most is exercise and you must not let them just go out for a walk!"* So I would ride out with this servant named Anfus and try my best to exercise the horses.

Interestingly, I did learn a lot of Arabic this way, as Anfus would like to tell me the name of things as we rode along. Riding along with him close behind was not my idea, but I was not allowed to go alone. Anfus was an Arab and unlike most other servants, he had his wife living nearby in a mud hut. He was from a different tribe from the others, and stayed with us all the time we were in Iraq. He would take the 3 horses to meet us after riding long distances daily. In my mind's eye, I can still see him riding the centre horse with one each side, with his chafia wrapped round his head and across his mouth to keep him cool. He would have to take some of the horses' food, and every 3 to 4 hours he would stop, put on the nose bags and then lie beside them himself, eating a kumbus rolled around hard boiled eggs and a couple of onions – or perhaps a few dates. This kumbus was a large flat thin bread – with no rising – and baked with a nice crispy top. It was very good indeed, with its flour being wholemeal, milled, grinded and refined by the women with a pestle and mortar.

Of our servants in Iraq, Miritch was the chief one and he

was with Ernest the whole 16 years that he spent there. Miritch was a wonderful person and came from the tribe near Rumaitha, where the two Sheiks Fahad and Braed were from, and were cousins or uncles. He looked after us in a wonderful way, ensuring that the others all did their jobs. It is hard to imagine now, but we had a lot of these man servants, and Miritch had an understudy called Abus, and there was also an Indian cook. Then we had a sweeper who also looked after the bathing. This meant fetching and heating the water in kerosene tins on a sort of bonfire in the garden. He also looked after the incinerator and burnt all the rubbish, which was a very important job because of flies and disease. I think this kind little man was Mohammedan, and he was kept busy by the other 'boys', as well as by myself.

We also had a 'Dobi', who I think was an Indian, who did all the washing and ironing. This was a full-time job because we changed our clothes so often in the heat.

At Diwaniyah in Iraq, there was a bathroom for each bedroom, but the baths were tin tubs and had to be filled and emptied by Mohammed. He would come along and say, *"Hamam hather, Sehile,"* which meant, *"Bath ready, Sir."*

Also, Miritch and Abus would wait at table, and when Ernest went out on inspection, he took Miritch and two others, Anwar and Kisoor. They were Railway employees and went with Miritch and did anything, messages, etc... Although it is hard to remember now what they would all have done, nevertheless it would have been very difficult for Ernest to do his work without them.

In summer, which was really hot for 9 months of the year, we slept out of doors; which meant that beds, blankets and pillows had to be often carried in and out, and up and down to the roof. Also, after we ate meals out of doors, tables and chairs were carried in and out. The daytime temperature was about 117 degrees Fahrenheit for months, and at night it was cold enough for a blanket.

We also had a gardener and his helper, as well as the groom Anfus, whom we saw as another friend. All these Arab men were polite, dignified and very efficient. Our ways were very strange to them and possibly the most strange was our women. At the time, the Arab woman was still veiled and never showed her face or went to other people's houses. In their own homes they did a lot of work, grinding the wheat, kneading the bread and staying away with the herds of animals sometimes for weeks on end, wherever there was grass in the desert. Ernest was very kind to all those people and got on very well with them all.

Please note that these memoirs of my husband's were recorded on tape, sometimes done in short outpourings of memory, and consequently the order of events was seldom chronological and often interspersed with humorous tales. As a result, a great deal of sorting had to be done and it seemed that I was the best person to do it, as I had lived through most of the story. My husband read and re-read the script, and the engineering details are exactly as he told it. His primary reason for writing these memoirs was to help young men who wanted to become engineers, although for him it was the only profession to choose, since he loved engineering inside out.

By telling the story of his many setbacks, he hoped to help these same young men to avoid many pitfalls, as well as learn the vital importance of gaining experience 'in the field' or 'on the job'. Perhaps at times some of his opinions (especially regarding engineering errors he witnessed) might seem slightly hard, but this was quite the opposite of his intention. Those involved were often his friends and there were no bad feelings. In a nutshell, his overarching concern with this book was that others might learn from his experiences.

To conclude, I often feel my husband Ernest was, in many ways, the ultimate bridge-builder, not just building bridges over rivers, but also building bridges between people, so that they might learn from each other and grow in friendship and kindness. In short, he was a bridge-builder in every sense.

Daphne Harpur

Post-script by Sally Harpur O' Dowd (niece of Ernest & Daphne Harpur)

In a strange coincidence, my auntie Daph was born at Fairholme, Monkstown, County Dublin. This house had been built about 100 years earlier in 1797 by the Reverend Singleton Harpur (Ernest's 4th time Great-grandfather). On the front doorstep of Fairholme is a mosaic of the Harpur Boar Crest. Auntie Daph was to grow up and then marry Ernest 25 years later and receive a beautiful ring with the Harpur Boar Crest.

Ernest during WW2

Printed in Great Britain
by Amazon

39862835R00119